STRAITJACKET

SOCIETY

Diagnosing the Madness of Modern Mental

Health Care

Guenevere MacDonald, PaMhA.

Published by:
Earth Harmony Living
Toronto, Quebec, Canada

ISBN: 978-1-990426-26-1

Disclaimer

This book is intended for informational and educational purposes only. It does not constitute medical, psychological, legal, or professional advice. The views and opinions expressed are those of the author and are based on research, historical records, professional consultation, and lived experience. Readers should seek appropriate professional guidance regarding any mental health, medical, or legal concerns.

While care has been taken to ensure accuracy, the author and publisher make no guarantees regarding the completeness or applicability of the information contained herein and assume no responsibility for errors, omissions, or outcomes resulting from its use.

First Edition, 2026

Printed in Canada

Dedication

This book would not exist without the people who stayed.

My ***family and friends****, thank you for standing by me.*

To those who offered perspective, encouragement, or quiet support along the way, thank you for showing up when it counted.

And finally, a special thanks to ***those who left****. Your absence clarified what mattered, who mattered, and why this book needed to be finished. In its own way, that mattered too.*

"But I don't want to go among mad people," Alice remarked.
"Oh, you can't help that," said the Cat: "we're all mad here."

Lewis Carroll, Alice's Adventures in Wonderland (1865)

"Be yourself; everyone else is already taken."

Oscar Wilde

Acknowledgments

A special thank you to all those who assisted in the writing of this book, including...

The many patients and their families, medical personnel, emergency responders, members of the criminal justice system and front-line community workers and volunteers. Without your input and support, this would not be possible. Thank you for sharing your professional and personal experiences.

Thank you to the organizations and agencies that guide, fund, and advocate for mental health, whose research, programs, and outreach directly informed this book:

- In the United States: *Substance Abuse and Mental Health Services Administration (SAMHSA), National Institute of Mental Health (NIMH), the 988 Suicide & Crisis Lifeline, National Alliance on Mental Illness (NAMI), Mental Health America (MHA), Active Minds, The Jed Foundation, Brain & Behavior Research Foundation, Bazelon*

Center for Mental Health Law, Mind Share Partners, National Association for Behavioral Healthcare (NABH), and countless community mental health centers and crisis support networks.

- In Canada: *Wellness Together Canada, Health Canada, the 988 Suicide Crisis Helpline, Canadian Mental Health Association (CMHA), Mental Health Commission of Canada (MHCC), Canadian Alliance on Mental Illness and Mental Health (CAMIMH), Kids Help Phone, Jack.org, the Institute for Advancements in Mental Health, Mental Health Awareness Foundation of Canada (MHAFOC), the Canadian Community Mental Health Network (CCMHN), and Library and Archives Canada,* whose records and research helped provide historical context for this book.

I'd like to extend a special thank you as well to the universities and research institutions whose scholarship, research, and guidance helped support the insights and content of this book – *Bishop's University (Sherbrooke, Quebec), Université de*

Sherbrooke (Sherbrooke, Quebec), Concordia University (Montreal, Quebec), University of Toronto (Toronto, Ontario), McGill University (Montreal, Quebec), University of British Columbia (Vancouver, British Columbia), University of New Brunswick (Fredericton, New Brunswick), Dalhousie University (Halifax, Nova Scotia), McMaster University (Hamilton, Ontario), University of Alberta (Edmonton, Alberta), Western University (London, Ontario), University of Glasgow (Glasgow, Scotland), King's College London (London, England), University of Oxford (Oxford, England), Harvard University (Cambridge, Massachusetts), Yale University (New Haven, Connecticut), Stanford University (Stanford, California), and University of California, Los Angeles (Los Angeles, California). Thank you for your pioneering work, your insights, and your willingness to share knowledge that made this book possible.

To the historians, archivists, and researchers whose work preserves the stories of mental health care and its evolution, your expertise, diligence, and dedication to truth provided the foundation for understanding the past and shaping the insights of this book.

Finally, to every single person working within the system, from the dedicated doctors, and nurses to the hardcore support staffs, whether you run programs, answer phones, write policies, listen with care, or share your story, thank you. Thank you for showing up, for refusing to look away, and for believing in the people society often forgets. Your input, your expertise, your histories, and your dedication to the lives of others have shaped us all in ways that cannot be overstated.

Contents

Introduction

The straitjacket: two arms pinned forever against your chest, a simple canvas tuxedo for madness, yet nothing galvanizes an audience like naming it in polite company. Watch faces blanch, eyebrows shoot skyward, lips tighten. Why? Because the straitjacket is our century's scarlet letter, a visceral souvenir from an era when "care" meant crushing wills and "treatment" meant theatrical cruelty. Back then, you needed buckles and leather to force compliance. Today? We've swapped the hardware for holy-sounding policies, diagnostic labels, funding formulas, and done a far sleeker job of locking people up in plain sight.

Sure, we like to say that the dark chapter is closed. No more walls as tall as small buildings. No more canvas corsets. We've softened our words. We've lowered the bars. But the impulse that birthed the straitjacket, the burning itch to manage anyone who makes us uncomfortable, hasn't gone anywhere. It just graduated to a new wardrobe. Now it is disguised as efficiency, "best practices," risk-management protocols and mental health "re-enablement" plans. And because everyone applauds a "compassionate" system, it's harder than ever to point out we're still corralling inconvenient minds.

This book drags those invisible straitjackets into the harsh light you've been avoiding. We'll stumble through the corridors of history, forgotten asylums where moral philosophy masqueraded as medicine; deinstitutionalization's broken promises; the rise of psychopharmacology that traded chains for pills; the slick takeover by private interests; and the alarming routinization of criminal justice as the catch-all for mental distress. At every juncture, we hailed progress. At every turn, new shackles quietly slithered into place, always sold as reform, always stamped "for your own good."

Let's be clear: I'm not here for a highbrow lecture or a finger-wagging sermon. This is as much your story as mine. I've slept in waiting rooms that smell like bleach and despair, squinted through the narrow slits of seclusion rooms, and heard the clinical click of diagnostic labels slapping shut around vulnerable lives. I've watched families chase elusive support while systems designed to "help" pile on mile after mile of red tape. I've seen clinicians, bless their scrubs, doing heroic work, while simultaneously being hamstrung by structures that prize speed, compliance, and liability avoidance over genuine care.

Nobody here is the villain. Well, maybe there are a few. Sure, everyone starts out with good intentions and a goal-driven philosophy of making the world a better place. Good intentions don't matter when the architecture you build tests people's patience, dignity, and very personhood. A nice label for everyone's favourite horror: containment masquerading as understanding.

So, who should crack open these pages? Clinicians who still believe they're in the business of healing. Policymakers dreaming of soundbites that end in "progress." Advocates waving reform banners. Families who've swallowed the comforting myths that everything's getting better. And you, the curious onlooker who'd rather hold onto a cozy illusion than confront harsh truths. Be warned: these chapters will unsettle you. They might make you furious. They'll nearly guarantee you can't pretend you don't know what's happening anymore.

If you find yourself itching for more, uneasy at what you'll discover, perfectly discomforted, then congratulations, you're exactly the reader this book was made for. Because the real straitjackets never went away. They just became invisible, and that's the most dangerous trick of all.

Chapter One
The Shadowed History of the Straitjacket

The straitjacket wasn't born in some gothic dungeon or conjured by medieval torturers with gleaming iron instruments. It sprang to life in the cold, rational glare of Enlightenment thinking, less a stroke of medical genius than an outgrowth of collective unease. Its purpose was blunt and unwavering: immobilize bodies, silence minds, and repackage subjugation as "care."

In the cramped asylums of the eighteenth and nineteenth centuries, canvas and buckles became the universal shorthand of authority. Strap someone down, and you delivered a message louder than any proclamation: "I hold power; you do not." Power, however, was never distributed equally. The poor, women labelled hysterical, racialized patients, nonconformists, political dissenters, these were the bodies most eagerly bound. The straitjacket functioned as both a physical restraint and a cultural branding, signalling to inmates, staff, and visiting philanthropists that these individuals were untrustworthy and unworthy of autonomy.

Origins were as bland as bureaucracy itself. In 1753, England rolled out an "arch device" of sturdy canvas and iron buckles, officially dubbed the "jacket" by reformers eager to distance themselves from their medieval predecessors. France followed in 1772, and soon the jacket became part of the institutional repertoire across Europe and North America. Prior to this "upgrade," treatment looked like little more than leather straps, chains, and manacles, simple but effective tools for shutting mouths and freezing limbs. The Enlightenment's term for the new design was "refinement."

By the early nineteenth century, the straitjacket had graduated from an emergency measure to a default setting. Mad-doctors and moral therapists alike extolled its virtues. Supposedly, it calmed the "disturbed" mind; functionally, it guaranteed order. Dayrooms once filled with restless pacing, loud shrieks, and convulsive gestures were emptied into padded cells or yards where all movement ended. In between these eras of stillness, some asylums boasted ‘therapeutic’ routines, forced labour in laundry rooms, regimented walks in walled courtyards, diet restrictions, and religious exhortations. Under the watchful eyes of attendants, violence was avoided at the cost of dignity. Clinical notes celebrated “tranquillity,” though inmates’ faces grew hollow.

Take the Broadmoor Asylum in England, circa 1860. Records show that as many as 60 percent of patients spent a minimum of four hours daily in restraints. At New York’s Bloomingdale, physicians praised the canvas design for preventing self-harm. Yet no mention appeared of the bruises beneath, the cramped joints, the terror so acute that suicide attempts sometimes followed release from the jacket’s merciless grip. To reformers, these were unfortunate side effects, collateral rather than central to the methodology.

Mid-century developments only deepened the practice. Industrialization demanded predictability; social chaos, especially among the indigent, represented a threat. The asylum, once billed as a refuge, transformed into a factory of compliance. Workhouses and penitentiaries borrowed the straitjacket model. Moral therapy gave way to mechanized routine: Stop moving. Stop speaking. Stop being inconvenient. In the name of progress, compassion was strapped tightly to a post, never to be heard from again.

The dawn of the twentieth century ushered in a new era: scientific psychiatry. Lobotomy, insulin shock, and electroconvulsive therapy each promised a more "modern" solution. Yet beneath this veneer of novelty churned the same impulse: control over care, restraint masquerading as remedy. When mechanical devices seemed archaic, doctors and administrators turned to chemicals. Barbiturates, bromides, and chlorpromazine arrived in childproof bottles, their labels promising "stabilization," "symptom management," or the even more euphemistic "chemical calming."

In theory, medication should have opened doors to conversation, empathy, and realigned brain chemistry sufficiently to allow meaningful dialogue. In practice, it all too often locked doors shut. Doses escalated until compliance was virtually guaranteed. A small warning might read: "May induce emotional blunting, compliance, and the slow evaporation of self." The "chemical straitjacket" mutes patients from within rather than without. Agitation falls silent, dissent becomes a memory, and the individualized human beneath the diagnosis dissolves into clinical statistics.

By mid-century, the canvas straitjacket and high-intensity electroshock found new bedfellows in the booming pharmaceutical and insurance industries. In the United States, the Hill-Burton Act funded sprawling state hospitals, even as managed care lobbied for shorter stays and cost-cutting diagnosis caps. Today's straitjacket wears steel-toed boots, sports a company logo, and grins from behind an intake desk. It's less canvas than policy, less buckles than bureaucracy, yet its grip can be just as unyielding.

Modern restraint arrives cloaked in forms and protocols: a forty-seven-page intake package, a six-month waitlist for therapy, a polite "call back next Tuesday," and the realization that help, if it ever arrives, will arrive on someone else's timetable. Lost referrals, shuttered programs, contradictory eligibility criteria, these are the invisible straps that leave no bruises but achieve the same outcome: control maintained, responsibility deflected, the individual quietly erased. Crisis becomes calendar fodder, distress, and an administrative inconvenience.

This device reveals more about us than it does about the patients. It exposes our compulsion to control, our terror of unpredictability, our addiction to quick fixes, our fear of vulnerability. In headlines and polite society, "mental illness" still reads as "dangerous" or "unhinged." That tidy caricature justifies neglect and underfunding, and let us never forget the prisons and jails teeming with those labelled "mentally ill" who simply never found another institution willing to take them in. Headlines feed the fear: an "unhinged" patient, a violent outburst, a tragedy spun to fit the trope. The canvas might vanish, but the stereotype stays cinched tight, squeezing empathy until it gasps.

Language itself has learned to restrain. Disagreement becomes "lack of insight." Questioning treatment is "noncompliance." Resistance gets recoded as "agitation." With administrative efficiency, every challenge to authority is pathologized, every flicker of autonomy stamped out before it even breathes. A patient dares to say "no"? The chart dubs it "uncooperative," and the physician orders a higher dose. Voices once calling for nuanced understanding now dissolve into box-checking and metric-gathering.

Widen the lens, and you see the straitjacket stitched into the entire system: broken funding, burned-out staff, overcrowded wards, police as default first responders, emergency rooms doubling as psychiatric lockups, rehospitalization rebranded "inevitable." Community mental health centers were meant to replace asylums but now struggle under bureaucratic mandates and budget slashes. Case managers juggle impossible caseloads; social workers wring their hands; families cry out for help that trickles in too late and too little.

In low and middle-income countries, the picture grows even starker. Shantytown clinics with no record-keeping, traditional healers wielding herbs and shackles, families chaining loved ones in the name of protection from self-harm. The global south's inherited asylum systems, left over from colonial regimes, linger half-abandoned, with patients often left to rot behind locked doors. The straitjacket here is made of neglect, the buckles of corruption, the straps of resource scarcity.

But let us not pretend that wealth guarantees freedom. Even in Europe and North America, private institutions slip in sedation so subtle it goes unnoticed. A sedative before lunchtime therapy, a knockout pill on discharge, financial incentives tucked into formularies. Pharmaceutical companies churn profit as patients trade consciousness for calm. The narrative remains the same: Control over care, chemistry over curiosity.

Stigma is the straitjacket's ever-faithful shadow. Employers question job applicants with past diagnoses. Landlords deny tenancy. Schools label students "difficult," suspending rather than supporting them. In every corner of society, mental health is the one place where suspicion, mistrust, and fear are as common as misplaced compassion. The societal buckle clicks shut before the patient ever enters the doctor's office.

Medicine, law, policy, and public opinion have each contributed their stitch to this garment. Guardianship laws strip adults of decision-making power; forced outpatient treatment demands medication compliance under threat of involuntary commitment. Psychiatric advance directives exist in theory but rarely in practice. In courts, judges rely on DSM entries as if they were immutable truths rather than contested categories. Every lever of authority, from state hospitals to street cops, becomes another clasp on the patient's wrists.

And yet, beneath the weight of these layered restraints, voices edge their way through. Activists who survived the giant wards speak of peer-run crisis centers, respite houses, and trauma-informed care that honours autonomy rather than extinguishing it. They point to Open Dialogue in Finland, where family and community replace locked doors, and medication is an option rather than a mandate. They celebrate psychiatric survivors who write their own narratives and shape policy from the grassroots.

These countercurrents remind us that the straitjacket is not inevitable; it has a history, and every history can be rewritten. Understanding its lineage, canvas to chemical, buckles to bureaucracy, forces us to ask the question every administrator dreads: Are we here to help people heal, or simply to find fancier, more palatable ways to keep them quiet?

The shadowed history of the straitjacket remains not as a dusty museum exhibit but the blueprint for modern mental healthcare. The canvas may be gone, but the impulse it embodied, fear of the unpredictable, hunger for control, care as secondary, is alive and well. Unmasking it demands more than sympathy; it requires systemic reform, redistributing power from institutions to individuals, prioritizing compassion over compliance, humanity over hierarchy.

Then, perhaps, we cut through the red tape, loosen the administrative buckles, and offer true sanctuary. Only then can care become a dialogue, instead of a directive; treatment becomes a collaboration, not a takeover; healing becomes a journey, rather than confinement. That is the challenge before us, one stitched into every form, every policy, every pill bottle that bears the faint echo of that first canvas straitjacket. To meet it, we must reckon with history, dismantle the devices, both physical and procedural, that bind us, and imagine a practice of mental healthcare unchained from fear.

Chapter Two:
The Enlightenment Era

So, let's slip into the candlelit grandeur of the so-called Age of Reason, a golden era of powdered wigs, lace cuffs, manicured salons, and ceaseless tea parties where the clink of porcelain echoed the clatter of new ideas. It was a time when coffeehouses buzzed with debates over Locke's tabula rasa, Newton's orbiting apples, and Kant's categorical imperatives. Enthusiasts proclaimed that humanity stood on the brink of perfection, that with enough logic and empirical rigor we could reorganize society like a well-oiled clock. Yet behind the polished syllogisms lurked a profound terror: anything that didn't fit neatly into the new rational order was instantly suspect. And nothing rattled the Enlightenment quite like madness, the glitch in humanity's operating system.

Philosophers such as John Locke, Isaac Newton, and Immanuel Kant argued that reason could perfect individuals and society. Locke taught that the mind was a blank slate, ready to be inscribed with knowledge; Newton described a universe governed by predictable laws; Kant insisted that moral action sprang from pure practical reason. If reason was civilization's shining foundation, madness became an existential fissure, a house of cards waiting to collapse under the slightest gust of unpredictability. Call someone "irrational," and suddenly they were not merely wrong but dangerous: a ticking time bomb in the drawing-room of progress. Studying them was scientific. Restricting them was a patriotic duty. Containing their capriciousness was the price of collective sanity.

Concurrently, the body shed its divine aura and was recast as a mechanical contraption. René Descartes and his intellectual heirs placed the mind in the machine's control room, ready to tinker whenever its gears ground awry. The body became the chassis, the nerves the wiring, and the brain the engine. When that engine overheated, when the mind "crashed," the Enlightenment's prescription was simple: apply order. Sometimes gentle, occasionally theatrical, but more often harsh and unyielding. Thus emerged the straitjacket, a hybrid of medical apparatus and disciplinary tool, its strapped canvas was a visual assurance that chaos could be securely buckled down.

Public demonstrations of control played well in salons and lecture halls. In Paris, Philippe Pinel famously strode into the Bicêtre asylum in 1792 and removed the iron chains that bound inmates, treating them like criminal suspects. His "moral treatment" replaced bondage with routine: daily walks, quiet conversation, humane meals. Yet behind the applause lay the same premise: the "insane" must still be corralled, observed, and kept from disturbing the public order. Over in York, England, William Tuke's Quaker retreat adopted a gentler façade, fresh air, productive work, kindness, but always under strict supervision. Both reformers softened the edges of brutality without challenging the central tenet: those deemed mad could not be trusted with freedom.

As medical science progressed, the urge to classify became irresistible. Physicians carved madness into neat diagnostic boxes, melancholia, mania, hysteria, general paresis of the insane, each label promising an elegant taxonomy. Cross the invisible line from sane to insane, and autonomy was forfeited. Biographies gave way to case files; individuality dissolved into standardized data. The straitjacket sat at the system's core, its strapped canvas shouting: Reason lost. Order imposed.

This obsession with rationality bled into political theory through the social contract. According to theorists like Hobbes and Rousseau, individuals willingly traded certain liberties for the security of the state. All well and good, unless your mind was "broken," in which case the contract was declared void. Your rights were suspended, and the asylum inherited the state's power to lock you away for your own "good." The contract between citizen and sovereign crumpled at the asylum door.

In the Enlightenment hierarchy, rationality perched grandly atop a pedestal; madness slid toward childishness and moral failure. Persons in mental distress were no longer seen as individuals in pain but as threats to the social body. The straitjacket became the ultimate symbol of chaos tamed, a declaration that restraint was not cruelty but civilization asserting itself. Imposing straps were proof that society held fast to its shining standards.

Philosophical debates over mind and body only strengthened the case. If mental "gears" jammed or short-circuited, immobilization seemed logical; forceful calm promised restored order. Crude and uncomfortable, yes, but impeccable in theory. And the public believed it was progress, not propaganda.

Discipline even shaped architecture. Asylums, prisons, and workhouses sprouted from the same blueprint: long corridors of locked doors, observation galleries, and central monitoring stations. Jeremy Bentham's Panopticon concept, with its watchtower peering into every cell, exemplified the era's faith in surveillance and efficiency. With chronic understaffing and no real therapy or medication, physical restraint was the most reliable solution. The asylum morphed into a miniature ideal society, every motion regulated, every outburst suppressed.

Clinical records reveal the rest: the terror of waking to strapped limbs, the cold bite of canvas, attendants debating whether another night immobilized was warranted. Patients recounted hours stretching into days, unable to move, eat, or relieve themselves without permission. Physical pain was brutal, but the psychological harm ran deeper; identity dissolved, agency evaporated, hope withered.

Women's accounts ring especially chilling. Sarah, confined in the early twentieth century for "nervous exhaustion" born of marriage, household drudgery, and social strain, later described the jacket as punishment for speaking, crying, or merely existing beyond silent compliance. Another patient, dubbed Mary, admitted for "melancholia," recalled attendants applying the straps with clinical efficiency, not to calm but to silence her screams. Under the guise of care, their autonomy, privacy, and very selves were stripped away.

By the late nineteenth century, asylums ballooned into overcrowded bureaucracies. Built for dozens, they housed hundreds; staff-to-patient ratios rendered genuine treatment impossible. The straitjacket endured not because it healed, but because it managed, neatly, predictably, safely. And when survivors walked free, many carried a phantom jacket in their minds, fabric triggers that provoked panic, and an authority that still inspired dread.

Class shaped compassion. The poor endured rigid discipline with minimal comfort; the wealthy sometimes received kinder "moral treatment" in private retreats complete with landscaped gardens. Yet kindness always had an edge: compliance earned privileges, deviation prompted correction. Freedom became something to be earned through good behaviour, not a birthright granted equally.

By the mid-twentieth century, deinstitutionalization movements and the advent of psychiatric drugs made the straitjacket less visible. Yet the underlying logic of control persisted, merely refined into subtler forms, locked units, seclusion rooms, sedating medications, endless risk-assessment paperwork. The tool changed, but the machinery endured.

The Enlightenment and the asylum left us with a legacy of care entwined with coercion. Stripped of its straps, the straitjacket's symbolic grip persists in modern policies and protocols that still equate difference with disorder. We did not abolish restraint; we simply learned to dress it up in kinder language. And in its newest guise, it is more dangerous than ever, because now we believe there is nothing left to resist.

Chapter Three
The Modern Pharmaceutical Straitjacket

Welcome to the age of the chemical chokehold. Today, the first, and often the only step in treating mental distress, is to slap a label on a patient and reach for a prescription pad. Antidepressants, antipsychotics, mood stabilizers, sedatives, anxiolytics: the parade of pills has grown so relentless that doctors reflexively dose before they even look. Rather than a thoughtful choice, medication is the default, administered with mechanical speed, defended with clinical fervour, and hailed as an unquestionable advance. Yet these drugs are barely out of medical infancy. They sprinted into practice and were subsequently normalized before their long-term fallout was understood. In the grand sweep of healing traditions, they are an experiment: quiet, ubiquitous, rarely challenged once they proved useful for maintaining order.

It all began, or so the story goes, in the bright hopes of the early 1950s. Enter chlorpromazine, baptized Thorazine, the chemical miracle that silenced voices, stilled delusions, and pacified the agitated. Wards that once echoed with anguished cries fell eerily quiet. Staff exhaled. Institutions swelled with the self-congratulatory notion that suffering had met its match. For some, it was a godsend; for others, a nightmare cloaked in triumph.

Families peered through the bars and glimpsed salvation. Suddenly, the asylum walls no longer seemed unbreakable. Patients once deemed incurable could be chemically subdued, stability recast as progress, sedation sold as compassion. Whether a person thrived or merely appeared tranquil ceased to matter; compliance replaced wellness. In the new vernacular, calm was cure enough.

Then came the cascade: antidepressants promising to banish despair, anxiolytics pledging to snuff out terror, mood stabilizers vowing to iron out every emotional wrinkle. Each influx arrived dressed in white-coat authority and crowned with media acclaim. But the real triumph wasn't understanding the human mind; it was managing it. Control seeped into the language: treat the symptom, ignore the source. Success became measurable output, attendance at work, muted outbursts, and a neatly assembled life that looked normal from the outside.

Behind the celebratory headlines, however, lurked a darker truth. As clinicians grew enamoured with pharmacology, they pushed therapy, social services, and community funding into the shadows. Pill counts fit billing codes and clinical guidelines, but building affordable housing did not. Medication was efficient and neat; real support required time, money, and political will. So, the prescription pad replaced social reform.

Psychotropics morphed into both symbol and solution. With a few milligrams, institutions could pretend the system functioned. Relapses were blamed on patient negligence, missed doses, lack of willpower, rather than the grotesque mismatch between human need and institutional apathy. When drugs dulled the signs of crisis, the crisis was deemed resolved. When they failed, the individual was deemed at fault.

Community care, once championed as the humane alternative to locked wards, was quietly hollowed out. The asylum did not vanish; it shrank into daily routines, strapped to wrists and hidden in orange pill bottles. The new chains were chemical, portable, invisible. And they demanded the same obedience.

By the 1960s and '70s, psychotropics burst into outpatient life. But while prescriptions flew, the networks to support them did not. Monitoring side effects, ensuring adherence, managing complications, all that burden shifted to patients and their families. Under the guise of "empowerment," responsibility was offloaded. What clinicians called freedom often felt like abandonment.

At home, relatives became untrained pharmacists, juggling bewildering regimens, watching loved ones slip in and out of lucidity. A missed pill meant recrimination; an adverse effect meant guilt. Families bore the weight of psychiatric care in silence, underfunded and under-resourced, while the institutions that had preached community support watched from afar.

And then there were the side effects.... oh, the side effects. Patients were told sedation was relaxation; tremors were “minor motor disturbances”; weight gain was a fair trade for stability; emotional flattening was called “therapeutic calm.” But these trade-offs weren’t minor. Pleasure, motivation, and identity all faded. Some victims of long-term use developed irreversible tardive dyskinesia, grotesque spasms that marked them forever as treated cases. Such horrors were dismissed as acceptable collateral damage, the price of a society more comfortable when its unquiet minds stayed quiet.

Despite the carnage, pharmacotherapy cemented itself as the cornerstone of mental health care. Medication was no longer one tool; it was the scaffold propping up a broken system. When community resources failed, chemistry was supposed to fill the gap. The promise of liberation from institutional walls turned out to be a promise to lock people into daily pill schedules, clinic visits, and endless monitoring.

This was the modern straitjacket: no leather, no metal, just a regimen of chemical compliance. Obedience equalled wellness. Skipping a dose didn’t invite curiosity or care; it triggered suspicion. “Off their meds" became a clinical verdict, stripping nuance from complex human suffering and replacing it with a binary of compliant or deviant.

Autonomy withered. Dosage and duration were decisions made in conference rooms, with patients granted little real input. Refusal wasn't reasoned dissent; it was "lack of insight," undermining a person's credibility. Distress wasn't a signal to adjust care; it was noncompliance, antithetical to the therapeutic regimen. Lives became a constant negotiation between what felt safe and what felt authentic, often at the cost of authenticity.

With each new class of drug, tricyclics, MAOIs, SSRIs, second-generation antipsychotics, the same script replayed: bravura claims of fewer side effects, grand promises of normalcy, all while the systemic failures persisted. Housing remained scarce. Jobs remained out of reach. Therapy remained underfunded. Pills managed symptoms but didn't correct the social conditions that created them.

More insidiously, the straitjacket shaped our very understanding of mental illness. Reduce everything to neurotransmitters, and the diagnosis becomes individual pathology. Social, environmental, and psychological roots vanish. Treatment turns into social regulation rather than genuine care. Invisible chemical bonds replaced visible bars, but punishment remained. Compliance was moral currency, currency that bought you acceptance. Miss a payment, skip a dose, and you were ostracized anew.

Education systems, workplaces, and even housing authorities adopted the chemical yardstick. Stability meant adhering to medication. If you played along, you passed muster. If you didn't, you became dangerous again. Society applauded the miracle of pills while ignoring the conditions, poverty, trauma, and isolation that medicine alone could never heal.

And yet, the miracle is real for many. For some people, medication lifts a crushing weight of despair or tempers storms of psychosis. Work, relationships, and daily life become possible when they might otherwise be impossible. Those benefits are not illusions. They are lifelines.

But lifelines carry a cost. Side effects linger, identities warp, and responsibility shifts away from institutions to individuals. Chemical stability too often substitutes for genuine freedom. Relief arrives entwined with restriction.

The tension between care and control is as old as psychiatry itself. We traded padded cells for plastic bottles and clinic doors. We swapped visible chains for the clandestine architecture of compliance checks and dosage charts. The hierarchy remained: those who prescribe, those who submit. Freedom remained conditional, tethered to a regime.

The straitjacket has only become more refined. It smiles from the pharmacy shelf and whispers from policy documents. It lives on in the assumption that 'normal' always means 'medicated'. It thrives on the idea that psychiatric disorders are defects to be corrected, rather than distress to be understood.

And still, the human spirit finds cracks. Peer movements, self-advocacy, and mutual support networks claim back a sliver of agency. They refuse to be defined solely by chemical charts and compliance scores. They demand a fuller conversation, one that includes therapy, community, and meaning.

So, let's unlock the door to today's asylum, the source of society's straitjacket. Not the one of padded cells and barred windows, but the one we carry pocket-sized in blister packs and clinic appointments. It is everywhere, quiet, pervasive, and normalized, and it still confines. The question is no longer whether we need medication. It is whether we will let it be the only answer.

Chapter Four
The Criminalization of Mental Illness

When the heavy iron gates of the asylums finally clanged shut, we patted ourselves on the back. We heralded an era of freedom, jubilantly sent the straitjacket to the museum, and congratulated each other on our enlightened progress. But the asylum never disappeared; it simply put on a new uniform. The peeling walls and padded rooms were swapped for fluorescent lights and patrol cars; the white coats traded for badges; medical consent quietly gave way to arrest warrants. Welcome to the modern asylum: no art therapy, no care plans, no real assessment, just handcuffs, a booking number, and the reassuring mantra: "We're here for your own good."

Deinstitutionalization was our crowning achievement. In the 1960s and '70s, governments celebrated the empty wards, cheered the shrinking hospital rolls, and forecast a bright future of community-based support. Psychopharmacology was supposed to liberate millions. Instead, we outsourced the problem, and then acted surprised when law enforcement stepped in. No beds, no clinics, no outreach teams? No matter. Police assume the role of gatekeepers to mental health, wielding nightsticks in place of empathy, orders instead of diagnoses.

A psychotic break becomes "disturbing the peace." A manic episode morphs into "disorderly conduct." A trauma flashback is recast as "resisting arrest." Requests for help? Labelled "noncompliance." The net result: where there once were padded cells and on-staff psychiatrists, we now have jail cells and detention officers. The coat may have changed, but the system's purpose remains: to isolate, to control, to lock away those who make us uneasy.

This isn't a bureaucratic "oops." It's precisely the design. Without a fully functional mental health system, law enforcement was beckoned onto center stage: conveniently, cheaply, and with zero specialized training. Police are taught to enforce laws, not to comfort or diagnose. But when community services collapsed, they became de facto crisis teams, armed with authority and force instead of compassion and therapy.

The statistics are damning. In many U.S. counties, jails and prisons have outstripped psychiatric hospitals in serving people with severe mental illness. More mentally ill Americans are behind bars than in all remaining inpatient psychiatric beds combined. Once inside, they confront overcrowding, chronic understaffing, and punitive routines, a veritable petri dish for worsening symptoms. Isolation cells, rigid schedules, mandatory lockdowns: none of it was designed for healing.

Time and again, incarceration transforms mental health crises into deeper pathologies. Therapy sessions vanish; medication becomes sporadic; trauma is reinforced, not relieved. Release is rarely a rebirth. Instead, ex-inmates return to the street with fewer resources, deeper scars, and often a new set of criminal charges. The revolving door spins, and society congratulates itself on "deinstitutionalization."

We must acknowledge who pays the highest price: the marginalized. Homeless individuals, people of colour, the uninsured, and those lacking a safety net are disproportionately swept up. Their distress, rooted in poverty, addiction, or prior trauma, is met with batons, tasers, and prison bars. The social determinants of health, such as stable housing, income, and community support, are ignored, while visible symptoms are punished.

On the street, a disoriented person wandering in pyjamas at dusk becomes "loitering" or "obstruction." Someone talking to unseen friends is a "public nuisance." An escape into silence or paranoia registers as "noncooperation." Each misinterpreted gesture, every frightened flinch, risks escalating into a physical arrest. Officers, fearing scrutiny, too often default to force. They must clear calls quickly, de-escalation takes time, and time is a luxury in precincts straining under budget cuts and staffing shortages.

The rhetoric around reform is slick: add a four-hour training module here, a "mental health liaison" badge there, and voilà, compassion achieved. Crisis Intervention Teams (CITs) are rolled out in select precincts and lauded as silver bullets. Yet adoption is spotty, evaluations are mixed, and most officers still receive little more than a cursory slide show on "diversion." When the adrenaline spikes and the public eye blazes, it's back to muscle over understanding.

In practice, psychiatrists' diagnoses become arrest charges. Mania is "assault." Depression is "failure to comply." Catatonia is "obstruction of justice." An officer's confidence can be mistaken for the truth, and training on cultural bias often plays second fiddle to directives: "Control the situation, protect property, keep bystanders calm." Human distress is recast as defiance.

Use-of-force policies compound the problem. In the name of legal prudence, officers learn to act quickly, pre-empting potential threats rather than waiting to assess. Handcuffs click on unresisting wrists as a precaution. Tasers are drawn to prevent "escalation." A physical takedown becomes the first, not last, resort. Each action ostensibly decreases liability, yet it deepens the chasm between crisis and care.

The numbers on fatal encounters are chilling. People with mental illness are sixteen times more likely to be killed in a police incident than others. In

2015, nearly half of all fatal police shootings involved someone in psychiatric distress. High-profile tragedies like the 2020 death of Daniel Prude in Rochester, New York, where mace and a spit hood turned a call for help into a fatal asphyxiation, underscore the lethal consequences of defaulting to force.

Looking at history, asylums once justified straitjackets and lobotomies as necessary control measures. Today, law enforcement justifies chokeholds and prolonged restraint as necessary. Both rationales rest on the same dark logic: "We did it to keep everyone safe." And both produce the same outcome: fear, injury, dehumanization. Handcuffs and pepper spray have become the modern levers of institutional neglect.

We stand at a crossroads. The danger is not that police officers are evil; it's that they never signed up to be mental health specialists. Just as we once recognized the cruelty of mechanical restraints, we must now reject the normalization of criminalizing distress. Real reform demands resources, not rhetoric: fully funded mobile crisis teams, 24/7 psychiatric hotlines, community drop-in centers, supportive housing, and guaranteed access to therapy.

Promising pilots exist. Eugene, Oregon's CAHOOTS program fields unarmed medics and mental health clinicians instead of officers, handling 20% of the city's crisis calls without a single shot fired. Toronto's Mobile Crisis Outreach Teams pair social workers with trained paramedics; their success in diversion and de-escalation has become a blueprint for humane response. These models show that empathy and expertise can replace force and incarceration.

Yet these exceptions lie eroded by limited funding, political rhetoric, and the inertia of tradition. We still underinvest in social services at levels that would make military spending blush. Meanwhile, policing budgets balloon. We pay police to patrol parks, streets, and malls, but leave gaping holes where mental health support should be.

Mental health courts and diversion programs offer glimmers of hope, early intervention, treatment mandates, and community supervision. But they remain underutilized, their capacity dwarfed by the ever-swelling jail populations. Without sustained commitment, these initiatives risk becoming window dressing on a system fundamentally built to punish rather than heal.

The sobering truth is this: criminalization of mental illness is neither accidental nor inevitable; it's the direct product of systemic neglect and policy choices. We decided that mental health was someone else's problem. We defunded, de-prioritized, then washed our hands as the police stepped in. Now, the asylum gates have swung wide once again, here on our streets, in our cells, under the glare of floodlights and in the echo of sirens.

The street-level straitjacket of policing grinds, and lives hang on by fragile threads. Every arrest, every forced restraint, every misread gesture inflicts trauma and erodes trust. Families carry the moral weight of watching their loved ones criminalized for pleading for help. Communities bear the social and financial toll of overfilled jails and hospitals. And public faith in justice unravels, one coercive encounter at a time.

Reform is possible if we treat mental health as infrastructure, not an afterthought. We must reallocate funds from incarceration to intervention, from patrol cars to crisis vans, from handcuffs to healing networks. We must demand universal access to care, continuous training in trauma-informed practices, and policies that enshrine de-escalation over detention.

Until then, the asylum doors remain open and revolving. Those who once languished behind barred windows now pass through armed checkpoints. Their pleas echo not in therapy rooms but in booking halls. The system stands as it always has, ready to confine, ready to control, ready to punish. And it waits, for the next crisis, the next arrest, the next life it will break.

Chapter Five
Societal Stigma: The Invisible Asylum Walls

Cages and cryptic statutes matter, yes, but what truly locks the doors is the way we see them. Even as science tore down ghosts and demons from the canon of madness, prejudice refused to die. It simply picked up a lab coat. Here's the hard truth: mental illness was pathologized, labelled, and categorized, but public perception remained rooted in fear, suspicion, and contempt. "Madness" still whispers of unpredictability, incompetence, and moral failure. Our language, the very tool we trust to free us, hammers another nail into the coffin of understanding. Words like "Lunatic," "insane," "psycho": all diagnostic convenience and social condemnation wrapped into one.

The modern era didn't exorcise these demons; it gave them better lighting. Hollywood scripts and 24-hour news loops teem with characters who wobble on the brink of violence or hysteria, reinforcing the notion that any deviation from the emotional norm equals threat. Even the rare sympathetic portrayal glazes its subjects in pity rather than granting them full humanity. We're offered spectacles of suffering rather than nuanced lives, and we swallow every spoonful.

And so, the walls remain, unseen yet unmoving.

When 50% of people with mental health conditions admit they've delayed or avoided treatment for fear of stigma, you begin to see how these invisible bars bite. Fear of judgment corrodes self-worth, morphs every mirror into an interrogation: Am I too broken to ask for help? Will they see me and recoil? The answer, society tells us, is "yes", unless we're willing to conceal our wounds behind a tidy mask of "wellness."

Even our most well-intentioned measures can swell the cell. Diagnostic labels are necessary for treatment protocols, but they flash neon signs above a person's head: DIFFERENT. DEFICIENT. Schools, workplaces, and families, clutching the idea of "protection", unwittingly replicate the custodial impulses of asylums past. They circumscribe harmless behaviours, impose low expectations, and spin protocols that read like shackles. Every glance of pity, every whispered assumption, every policy written without human dignity in mind, adds another brick to the wall.

The machinery of othering has two chambers: external and internal.

Externally, it hums in microaggressions and exclusion. A boss who balks at a disclosure of bipolar disorder, suspecting unreliability. A landlord who flinches when you mention therapy, fearing "liability." Friends who whisper "high-strung" or "too intense" rather than ask if you're okay. Communities that declare mental health taboo, shooing conversations into dark corners.

Internally, it becomes a mental prison. You learn to monitor your own words, suppress your moods, and anticipate every sideways glance. You rehearse explanations for yawns that linger too long, half-smiles that sag. You pre-emptively apologize for the war raging in your head.

Language is the lockpick that never shows up on a metal detector. When "crazy," "psycho," or "unstable" become punchlines, each utterance drills a nail in the coffin we're already buried in. We shrug off these slurs as harmless banter, never pausing to note that they breed fear and mistrust in every ear.

Structural stigma burrows deeper. Employment policies with undisclosed medical history clauses. Insurance forms that hike premiums on "pre-existing psychiatric conditions." Housing applications that ask if you've ever been "committed." Museums of microaggression are built into everyday forms and handbooks, each one a brick in the labyrinth.

And for those living at the crossroads of multiple oppressions, people of colour, LGBTQ+ individuals, immigrants, and the poor, stigma fuses with racism, xenophobia, and classism into a molten alloy of isolation. Indigenous and Black communities, for instance, face higher rates of misdiagnosis, overmedication, coercive interventions, and then watch as police stations and prisons become default treatment centers. These aren't separate struggles; they're concentric circles, each reinforcing the next.

It's a feedback loop: societal stigma discourages help-seeking; untreated conditions manifest as crises; crises are interpreted through prejudice; stereotypes are further entrenched. Stigma is both cause and consequence, a hall of mirrors that shrinks the space in which we dare to breathe.

Breaking the stigma requires more than policy tweaking or glossy awareness campaigns. It demands a social exorcism. We must cultivate empathy as a daily ritual, not a TED Talk bullet point. Education must be honest, adaptive, intersectional, addressing mistrust in Black neighbourhoods, multilingual barriers in immigrant communities, and cultural taboos in faith-based circles. Media accountability must be relentless: when the evening news leans on scare tactics, we call it out. When sitcoms turn depression into a punchline, we refuse to laugh.

Every public figure who names their own struggle cracks open a door. Every peer-support program that pairs lived experience with compassionate training shatters another bar. Intentional Peer Support, youth networks, mentorship circles: these are not feel-good add-ons but frontline soldiers in the war on stigma.

Open dialogue is our weapon of choice. Storytelling events, podcasts, social media threads where real voices speak without spin, these are the chisels we need. They chip away at the assumption that vulnerability is weakness. They carve out truth from the thick stone of prejudice.

Laws and programs can only scaffold change; they can't forge empathy. Real transformation happens in everyday interactions: the coworker who checks in after you've called in sick; the friend who resists the urge to say, "snap out of it," and instead listens; the stranger on a bus who doesn't recoil when you clutch your head in an anxiety surge.

Language builds prisons as surely as bricks do. If we all, at home, at work, on social media, refuse to tolerate jokes about "crazy" coworkers or "psycho" drivers, the walls begin to crumble. Every correction, every gentle refusal to repeat a stereotype, chips away at the asylum.

Silence is complicity. Speaking out is a responsibility. Change doesn't happen in grand gestures alone; it happens in the small defiance of a single voice.

Chapter Six
Employment and the Invisible Straitjacket

Stigma isn't content with nasty whispers; it moves into our workplaces and rents office space in our heads. Society pats itself on the back for "helping," yet those shiny revolving doors stay stubbornly locked whenever someone with a mental health history shows up. Then we politely reserve every opportunity for everyone else.

For people managing mental health conditions, finding and keeping a real job feels like navigating a labyrinth of bias, financial precarity, and the slow burn of self-doubt. Employment isn't only about paychecks. Work delivers purpose, routine, social connection, and identity, pillars of mental well-being that crumble when you're shut out. Yet the unemployment rate for serious mental illness hovers around 70–75 percent, compared to a mere 4–5 percent in the general population. This yawning gap isn't about ability; it's about decades of fearmongering, shadowy stereotypes, and the absence of basic mental health education in boardrooms.

Employers often clutch their pearls over "reliability" or "workplace safety," as if every person with depression or bipolar disorder is a ticking time bomb. Without training or real-life stories to counter the scare tactics, hiring managers rely on half-baked assumptions: that symptoms will flare unpredictably, that productivity will tank, that the entire office might implode. Microaggressions slip beneath the radar: "Are you sure you can handle this?" or the classic, "Must be one of your off days," paired with a knowing smirk. Promotions stall, evaluations skew negative, and accommodations become punishments in disguise.

Imagine spending every shift concealing your struggles, like a performer in a one-person disguise act. Stress accumulates. Sleep unravels. Medication schedules go out the window. You avoid asking for help because help feels like an admission of weakness. And with each passing month, the rungs on that corporate ladder feel ever more distant, your confidence erodes, and the paycheck you fought for loses its dignity. Burnout creeps in, relapse looms, and financial hardship tightens its grip.

What's lost when we lock out talent on this scale? The economy falters, deprived of creativity, fresh perspectives, and hidden strengths. Socially, we validate the old myths: mental illness equals incompetence, fragility, or danger. But evidence tells another story. Companies that embrace mental health training, inclusive policies, and supportive management see up to a 25–30 percent drop in absenteeism, along with spikes in morale, collaboration, and creativity. Inclusion isn't a charitable afterthought; it's a business imperative.

Changing the script demands more than sticking mandates in a handbook. Disability discrimination laws and mental health parity acts lay the groundwork, but they're toothless without real buy-in. HR seminars on legal compliance become pointless if managers still quiver at the thought of hiring someone who admits to therapy. Empathy can't be ticked off a checklist; it grows when people actually listen to colleagues who've navigated these challenges.

Peer support circles, mentorship networks, and designated safe zones transform whispered fears into honest conversations. Flexible hours or telecommuting options aren't just perks; they're lifelines that let people weather fluctuations in their health without losing their jobs. Phased returns after medical leave, confidential access to counselling, or simple workload adjustments demonstrate that productivity and compassion can share a desk.

Work is therapy when it offers routine and purpose; it's independence when it brings a stable income; it's community when it forges social ties. Every successful employment story chips away at the narrative that mental illness is synonymous with weakness. Inclusive workplaces shine a spotlight on potential, pushing other institutions, from schools to policymakers, to follow suit. Employment becomes a two-way street: it heals individuals and dismantles stigma.

But let's not pretend this fight happens on a flat playing field. Race, gender identity, sexual orientation, socioeconomic status, and geography all intersect with mental health, stacking barriers like a house of cards in a windstorm. A Black woman with bipolar disorder might face the twin terrors of racism and mental-health bias, from job interviews to on-the-job evaluations. Intersectionality means one-size-fits-all policies collapse under real life. We need targeted programs that address mental health stigma alongside systemic inequities.

Models like Individual Placement and Support (IPS) prove what's possible. In the U.S., people in IPS programs are twice as likely to land competitive employment as those in traditional vocational tracks. Key ingredients? Rapid job placement, personalized coaching, and ongoing ties to mental health services. It's a reminder that work can be both therapeutic and pragmatic when we invest in the right support.

The financial toll of exclusion dwarfs mere lost wages. Unemployment frays housing options, makes transportation a gamble, and limits access to healthcare. In the U.S., disability benefits can vanish if you earn even a modest paycheck, trapping people between a rock and a bureaucratic hard place. In Canada, universal healthcare cushions one blow, but high rents and scarce public transit still leave many teetering on the edge. For someone juggling medication costs, therapy copays, and travel expenses, every dollar is a test of priority, and a misstep can plunge them back into crisis.

The psychological fallout is equally brutal. Without work's structure and social contacts, isolation deepens. Self-esteem deflates under the weight of repeated rejection. Depression and anxiety sharpen their claws, and the risk of relapse spikes. Employment isn't an optional luxury; it's a cornerstone of recovery, bolstering resilience, agency, and dignity.

Supposed legal safeguards, the Americans with Disabilities Act, the Accessible Canada Act, promise protection. Yet savvy employers sidestep them with thin euphemisms: "not the right fit," "performance gaps," or "postponed accommodations." Proving discrimination becomes an expedition through dense legal thickets, where microaggressions and implicit bias leave almost no evidence trail.

Now, consider how housing and employment are two halves of the same broken whole. A secure home gives you a landing pad to job-hunt, attend appointments, and maintain health. A steady job ensures rent checks clear, and lights stay on. Remove one, and the other crumbles. But too many programs tackle housing and work separately, as if people can drink from one cup and fill the other later. Integrated services, combining supported housing with vocational coaching, yield better retention rates in both domains, smoother recoveries, and a real shot at autonomy.

Policy fixes and glossy pamphlets aren't enough. Real change germinates when decision-makers meet the humans behind the data. Lived-experience panels, story-sharing sessions, and honest town-hall forums force people to confront the person behind the label. Eye contact dismantles stigma faster than any mandatory training quiz.

Being shut out of employment does more than bleed bank accounts. It gnaws at the soul. Day after day, each rejection note feels like a verdict. Invisible barriers whisper, "You don't belong here." Anxiety blooms into shame. Confidence wobbles. Hope fades. And while the world insists work is an unquestionable right, it erects obstacle courses for those with mental health conditions, studded with bureaucratic hurdles and thinly veiled prejudice.

Below are real-world outcomes of targeted employment supports and support programs for individuals living with mental health challenges, numbers that should shame any business claiming inclusion:

• California, USA (Dept. of Rehabilitation, 2020): Employment Rate 58%; 65% retention at 1 year
• New York, USA (Individual Placement & Support, 2019): Employment rate 60%; 75% retention at 6 months
• Washington, USA (Housing First + Supported Employment, 2021): Employment rate 70%; retention data N/A
• Texas, USA (Workforce Commission, 2021): Employment rate 52%; 68% retention at 6 months
• Florida, USA (Vocational Rehabilitation, 2022): Employment rate 50%; 60% retention at 1 year
• Ontario, Canada (Employment Supports for Persons with Disabilities, 2022): Employment rate 55%; N/A
• Québec, Canada (Programme d'Aide à l'Emploi, 2020): Employment rate 52%; 68% retention at 1 year

• British Columbia, Canada (Employment Program BC, 2021): Employment rate 48%; 70% retention at 6 months

Even with promising stats, the blunt reality remains: a paycheck means little when you don't know where you'll sleep. Work can grant purpose and dignity, but without a home, it's a tightrope over an abyss of stress and instability. The next battlefront is clear: housing. For those contending with mental health challenges, the fight doesn't end at their workstation; it begins where they rest their head.

Chapter Seven
Housing, Stability, Stigma, and Survival

If employment is the foundation of independence, then housing is the crumbling wall that keeps it from caving in. You can train someone, coach them, even parade them onto a factory floor, but without a roof overhead, all that hope is just decoration. Job placement programs might promise renewal, peer support groups may patch a few cracks, but when your everyday reality is defined by rent due, eviction notices taped to your door, or makeshift tents under highway overpasses, even the most sterling recovery plan wobbles. Welcome to the fractured battleground where dignity, opportunity, and survival collide.

Housing is never just shelter. For people with mental health conditions, it's the arena where system neglect fights tooth and nail against urgent human need. Our "safety net" resembles Swiss cheese, utterly riddled. Think the painful employment gap is bad? Try combining a $12-an-hour wage with rents that spike faster than wildfire, landlords who screen out anyone with a scar on their credit history, and bureaucratic limbo that can swallow you for months. The result: paychecks vanish on rent, eviction squirms around every corner, and a mental health crisis waiting to happen finds fertile ground.

Between 2018 and 2022, Canada's Point-in-Time counts revealed a 20 percent increase in homelessness, and that's before you factor in the 36,058 people who were estimated to be chronically unhoused in 2024. Even aggressive reforms, touted in headlines, barely scratched the surface. Without policies that leap far beyond small fixes, homelessness will keep climbing as vulnerable groups, especially those wrestling with anxiety, bipolar disorder, schizophrenia, or depression, find themselves locked out of an ever-tightening housing market. Canada would need to roughly double annual housing starts over the next decade just to loosen the affordability chokehold. Yet current efforts barely nudge the dial.

Flip the coin to the United States, and the picture is equally grim: hundreds of thousands sleeping rough on any given night, and that number ticking upward as demand outpaces every half-hearted policy response. Sky-high rents thinly stretched safety nets, and labour market exclusion form a locked loop, no key, no escape, just the echo of desperation. In both countries, the public systems are designed to cradle people rather than push them into freefall.

Consider the numbers behind the human faces: in Canada, only about 46.8 percent of individuals with severe mental health disabilities have jobs, far below the general population. In the U.S., roughly 38 percent of adults with serious mental illness hold full-time work, compared to more than 60 percent of those without mental health challenges. That yawning gap is a canyon where opportunity goes to die. Behind every percentage point is a person: bouncing between friends' couches, terrified of another winter on the streets; someone who lost their job after disclosing their PTSD, then watched their apartment slip away when the rent rose by $200 overnight.

The cycle is relentless. Joblessness makes homelessness almost inevitable, and homelessness makes steady work a distant dream. You can't look for a job without an address, and you can't keep an apartment without a steady income, or so the merciless logic goes. Research in Canada shows that regions with higher local employment rates correlate with shorter durations of homelessness. Yet outside pockets of urban prosperity, opportunities are scarce, and the social safety net is full of holes big enough to swallow entire families.

Breaking this cycle demands a multi-layered assault. First, legal protections must be sharpened and enforced: anti-discrimination laws in housing and employment are essential, but they are utterly toothless without rigorous oversight. Then comes education, landlords, employers, and the general public need to understand that mental illness isn't a choice or a moral failing, but a medical reality that affects one in five adults each year. Fight implicit bias with training programs and frank conversations; rip down the stigma, brick by brick.

Next, expand structural supports:
Governments and communities need to integrate...
• Supportive housing, permanent, affordable units wrapped in on-site help, prove time and again that people stay housed longer when services are within reach.

• Rental assistance that moves beyond the scattered pilot projects to scale, delivering predictable subsidies to those who need them most.
• Vocational programs and individualized job coaching to give people the tools to navigate interviews, request workplace accommodations, and manage on-the-job stress.
• Peer support, the secret weapon, to empower individuals with mentors who've walked the same treacherous path, offering empathy, tactical tips, and a living testament that recovery and stability are possible.

Together, these pieces form a scaffolding for recovery, autonomy, and full social participation. Systemic reform guarantees fairness and opens doors; community support bolsters resilience; individualized aid addresses each person's unique history and hurdles. When aligned, these strategies can finally break the vicious cycles of marginalization and economic vulnerability, letting people not just survive, but also reclaim dignity and pursue ambitions.

Vocational rehabilitation programs stand out in the evidence. Participants in supported-employment models, where job development, placement, and coaching mesh seamlessly, are roughly twice as likely to land competitive roles compared to those in traditional services. Imagine doubling the employment prospects for a demographic that's often written off as unemployable. That's real impact. Better still, these programs integrate people into mainstream workplaces, chipping away at stigma in the office as much as in policy circles.

Peer support is the force multiplier. Mentors with lived experience bring razor-sharp insight and genuine empathy, modelling coping strategies and guiding newcomers through disclosure dilemmas and accommodation negotiations. Studies consistently show that peer involvement boosts engagement, confidence, and job retention. Lived experience isn't just a nice add-on; it's the bridge between clinical recovery and real-world success.

The gold standard emerges when vocational rehab is combined with housing supports, clinical care, and community services. Programs like Housing First in the U.S. and At Home/Chez Moi in Canada prove that stable shelter, coupled with job coaching and mental health services, fosters sustained independence, employment stability, and well-being. Policy levers, financial incentives for employers, inclusive workplace training, and accessible accommodations further amplify these wins.

But one-size-fits-all policies fail. Intersectionality must guide every step. Race, gender, sexual orientation, and socioeconomic status each intersect to compound barriers. Without targeted measures, we risk reinforcing the very inequities we claim to erase. Anti-racism training for employers, culturally and linguistically tailored services, mentorship for LGBTQ+ individuals, outreach to Indigenous communities, these are not optional extras, but lifelines.

Advocacy organizations and peer networks keep the momentum from stalling. They link people on the ground with policymakers, ensuring that laws and programs reflect real needs rather than theoretical ideals. Boosting their funding, infrastructure, and visibility means amplifying voices that have spent too long on society's margins.

Financial security is inseparable from housing and employment success. Expanding disability benefits, streamlining application processes, and integrating financial literacy into recovery plans is essential. A person who understands budgeting, debt management, and savings, matched with stable housing and supported job opportunities, is far less likely to spiral back into crisis.

Yet even the best-designed programs flounder without ongoing evaluation. We need robust data on employment rates, housing stability, income levels, mental health outcomes, and overall quality of life. Policymakers must pivot as labour markets shift, as remote work blends with gig-economy volatility, and as populations age. Proactive adaptation, not reactive scrambling, prevents new gaps from opening.

We have case studies at the provincial and state levels, each offering lessons, some brilliant, some cautionary. In British Columbia, a pilot project paired 200 people facing chronic homelessness with designated job coaches and peer mentors; six months later, 65 percent had stable housing and part-time or full-time work. In California, counties that increased rental vouchers by 30% saw a measurable dip in emergency shelter use within one year. These successes beg to be scaled, not studied to death behind government or university walls.

If stark numbers, human stories, and sobering stats haven't registered the alarm, I'll be blunt: society's approach to housing and employment for those with mental health conditions is a master class in bureaucratic cruelty and squandered potential. The blueprints exist. The programs exist. Yet every day, people are turned away at the door, boxed out of economic opportunity, or nudged back into instability by stigma, indifference, or inertia.

The next battleground isn't a new shelter or a fresh resume, it's education. Before someone can challenge discrimination or navigate the labyrinth of tenancy and job applications, they need the tools to understand what mental health truly entails: not the sensationalized caricatures fed by headlines, but the real, messy, human experiences behind each diagnosis. Schools, workplaces, and media must confront the myths, replace fear with knowledge, and fiction with lived reality. When society grasps the truth about mental health, it can stop feeling like a lottery ticket and become a right.

This is no feel-good manifesto. It's a call to arms. Peer support, vocational rehabilitation, and supportive housing are evidence-based lifelines. They work. Now, we need the political will, the public awareness, and the cross-sector collaboration to scale them, to move from pilot to permanent, from trickle to flood. Otherwise, we'll keep watching paychecks vanish, doors slam shut, and the same people bounce endlessly between crisis beds, welfare lines, and the rent-demand gauntlet.

The clock is ticking. The cracks in our systems deepen daily. We can pretend this is someone else's problem, or we can fight back, armed with data, compassion, and the messy, powerful force of lived experience. Those are our choices. And in the unforgiving calculus of housing instability and mental health, passivity is by far the cruellest verdict of all.

Chapter Eight
Education The Mental Health Divide
The Student Side of the Straitjacket

If employment is the foundation of independence, then education is the mould into which that foundation is poured, and for students contending with mental illness, that mould is rarely pristine. More often than not, it arrives cracked, warped, or actively hostile to any unpredictable fluid element. By the time résumés are discarded or rental applications are denied, the sorting has already taken place in classrooms that tout themselves as neutral engines of opportunity but, in practice, function as early-stage filters. This isn't a Harry Potter kind of sorting. Behind closed doors, schools quietly rank students by "manageability," by "giftedness," and, most damningly, by how simply they can be dismissed as too complicated to bother with.

Mental illness does not tiptoe into adulthood like an unannounced guest who failed to RSVP. It storms in early, often clumsily, always inconveniently, and usually at the precise moment when society least wants to deal with the fallout, on the playground, in the cafeteria, or under the fluorescent glare of a classroom. Motivational posters plastered on the walls insist that everyone is capable of success, but beneath those posters, distress thrashes and spills over, long before any formal diagnosis is handed down or acronyms take shape. Anxiety, depression, sensory overload, they simmer in the background, shaping how a child raises her hand, how a teenager eats lunch, how both calculate the risks of visibility.

For the most severe and persistent conditions, such as schizophrenia, bipolar disorder, and chronic mood disorders, the loudest symptoms often erupt during adolescence. Again, this is hardly a coincidence. Adolescence is a perfect storm: cognitive expectations spike, social pecking orders ossify, identity feels as brittle as spun glass, and the brain itself undergoes relentless remodelling. What might have been dismissed at ten as "eccentricity," "moodiness," or "attention-seeking" by age fifteen has become impossible to ignore when grades crater, friendships evaporate, or perception itself begins to fracture. Teachers cling to euphemisms like life preservers, whispering about "motivational issues" or "attitude problems" instead of naming the mental health crises unfolding in their own classrooms.

Hormones and attitude are often pinpointed as the main culprits, but the true origin story rarely begins at puberty. In retrospect, many adults living with serious mental illness can pinpoint warning signs in the haze of childhood or pre-adolescence: chronic, at-times paralyzing anxiety; emotional outbursts so explosive they border on rage; hypersensitivity to sounds or textures that render classrooms a minefield; attention that flickers out like a faulty lamp; social withdrawal that feels safer than the bullies in the hallway. These early indicators rarely conform to tidy diagnostic categories, so the education system repackages them into more digestible forms, behavioural disruptions, effort deficits, attitude issues, the perennial scapegoat: "bad parenting." The child is never ill; the child chooses to behave poorly. And once that narrative is in place, support transforms seamlessly into discipline, and care is recast as correction.

From the first day of kindergarten, the classroom is primed to function as an informal containment site. Deviations from the "norm" are managed rather than understood. The implicit curriculum teaches students not how to identify their distress or seek appropriate help but more often than not how to internalize shame, mask symptoms, and perform "normal" just well enough to slip by without consequence. Thus, the first invisible straitjacket slides on: a cheap, unspoken restraint that chafes the shoulders but keeps the arms pinned. That shackle is in place long before any adult ever utters the phrase mental health.

The effects accumulate, compounding like hidden interest on a loan. A child's academic struggles are read through a lens of laziness or, on the far opposing end of the spectrum, through overachievement. Social withdrawal is stamped "antisocial." Emotional dysregulation is coded as defiance. Each mislabel, each punitive referral, each admonishment chips away at self-worth and self-trust. The level of disturbance, participation, failure or bookworm science club status frequently rates its severity. By the time a formal diagnosis finally arrives, if it ever does, the student has already internalized that seeking help is tantamount to self-sabotage, and that any display of vulnerability will be met not with compassion but with suspicion and punishment.

Even for the few who manage to raise their hands and voice their struggles, the educational apparatus offers precious little in the way of genuine support. School-based mental health services vary wildly by district. In some places, a lone counsellor, tasked with hundreds of students, tries valiantly to field referrals and mediate crises. In others, itinerant psychologists flit between schools, their schedules so congested that students face waiting lists measured in months. Referrals to external specialists too often disappear into bureaucratic black holes. The most common "accommodations" consist of a flimsy pamphlet or a checklist of referral numbers, shoved into trembling hands with the unsaid addendum: Good luck, you're on your own.

As students advance to post-secondary institutions, the illusion of independence only magnifies the problem. Universities boast glossy brochures featuring yoga mats under cherry blossom trees and coffee carts offering matcha lattes in the student union. They advertise "holistic well-being" centres with photos of serene counsellors and promise "24/7 mental health support." But behind the polished façade, reality diverges sharply. Counselling centers buckle under the weight of demand. Waiting periods for initial appointments can stretch to weeks or even months. Group therapy sessions are rationed like luxury goods. The unstated message resonates clearly: your distress is an inconvenience to our schedule. Please contain it privately or risk academic failure. And if you fail, it's your fault for being too needy, too fragile.

These systemic failures warp student culture. In the absence of robust, readily available support, stigma thrives in the shadows. Asking for help is recast as a sign of weakness or immaturity. Disclosure becomes a strategic gamble. Will this professor understand, or will this administrator write you off? Meanwhile, academic expectations grow ever steeper, pressuring students to produce ever more stellar GPAs and flawless portfolios while simultaneously hiding any sign of vulnerability. It's little wonder that when distress builds unchecked, manageable conditions metastasize into full-blown crises. Students burn out on a mass scale, drop out in secret, or vanish entirely, and institutions feign surprise each time it happens.

When schools abdicate their responsibility for mental health education, students do not simply surrender. They increasingly turn to the Internet. Social media platforms, self-styled wellness influencers, peer anecdotes, and algorithm-driven content become the primary instructors in mental health literacy. According to recent surveys, over half of adolescents actively search online for information on depression, anxiety, and self-care strategies. Many encounter diagnostic terminology before grasping the nuances of context and severity. They adopt self-diagnosed labels like badges of identity before any professional evaluation. They sift through a deluge of stigma-laden caricatures, "crazy," "manic pixie," "triggered princess", before finding any accurate portrayal. No wonder they emerge from these digital classrooms with fractured understanding and a cocktail of self-help advice that can sway from evidence-based mindfulness to potentially harmful "nootropics" pushed by unscrupulous marketers.

This digital churn is not a reflection of youthful recklessness. Rather, it underscores the void left by educational institutions that refuse to provide structured mental health education. In the classroom's silence, algorithms roar. Schools warn about "dangerous misinformation," yet offer no cohesive, evidence-based alternative. It's as if they're saying, "Don't believe what you see online." Also, "We're too busy or understaffed to guide you through what's real." It is the modern-day equivalent of Gen X's introduction to Sex Education. Today's students benefit from the persistent demand for correct and updated sex education in schools, thanks to their predecessors, while simultaneously experiencing the same information blockade in mental health education. Irony.....

And yet, the data is irrefutable: when mental health education is integrated deliberately into school curricula, student outcomes improve measurably. Classrooms that include structured lessons on emotional regulation, stigma reduction, and help-seeking behaviours see fewer disciplinary incidents, higher rates of counselling utilization, and improved academic performance. Peer-led programs decrease bullying related to mental health by up to 30 percent. Early recognition and intervention reduce the likelihood of crisis-level episodes. Countries that mandate social-emotional learning in elementary grades report lower teen suicide rates and increased graduation rates. This is not theoretical; it is demonstrable, actionable progress.

Of course, education alone does not cure mental illness. No amount of classroom instruction will remake a shattered neurotransmitter system. But ignorance, left unchallenged, guarantees damage. A student who has never heard of cognitive behavioural strategies may endure panic attacks in isolation. A child who has never seen bipolar disorder discussed without sensationalism may endure manic episodes in secret. A teen who believes depression is a moral failing may never reach for the lifeline of professional care.

For students, the mental health divide is not an abstract policy debate. It is a daily ordeal lived in missed classes, in trembling hands popping open the locker to retrieve books, in panic surges when exams loom, in referrals to the principal's office for "defiance" that was really a symptom flaring uncontrollably, and in the countless moments when the safest choice is to retreat into silence. Institutions call it education. Students call it survival. Somewhere in that expanse, mental health is consistently ignored, and the invisible straitjacket tightens.

And it continues to tighten inch by invisible inch, until one day the student stands at the edge of the campus quad, staring out. Behind them are years of forced compliance, of contorted performances of normality, of whispered reprimands and shaming glances. Ahead is a future they've been conditioned to see as either flawless success or absolute failure, with no room for the messy, unpredictable spectrum of human experience. The straitjacket of ignorance has seeped into every fibre of their academic life, and now it's beginning to define their very identity.

Chapter Nine
Education The Mental Health Divide
The System That Fails Everyone

If students are the casualties, the education system is the terrain where damage becomes not just likely but architecturally inevitable. Picture a scarred battlefield, strewn with bodies, each bearing wounds both obvious and hidden. Now imagine that the only "first responders" on site are expected to diagnose and triage without training, supplies, or even the basic protocols paramedics, social workers, or therapists rely on. That, in a nutshell, is modern schooling.

Teachers stand at the frontline, handed a clipboard instead of a medical kit, a bell schedule instead of a triage protocol. They're the sentries of adolescent suffering: if a student crumbles under anxiety, if someone snaps at a peer out of trauma, if another drifts into a fog that might be emerging psychosis, teachers are told to notice, flag, and keep the day rolling. Observe everything, understand nothing, and above all, never let the learning stop.

This is not negligence born of malice; it is negligence by design. Educator preparation programs allocate, on average, fewer than five contact hours to mental health beyond "classroom management strategies." There's a cameo on bullying, a brief role-play on de-escalation, and maybe a 45-minute primer on recognizing suicide risk. Then it's back to phonics, fractions, and the miracle of student engagement. The message is crystalline: witness distress, file a form, and move on.

Teachers are not clinicians. They're not psychologists who can distinguish PTSD from defiance or anxiety from sheer disengagement. They're given no diagnostic manuals, no therapeutic toolkits, no safety nets. Yet with class sizes aching past thirty, budgets deflating year after year, and zero margin for error, they're routinely asked to step into those roles anyway. What follows is instinct, sometimes brave, sometimes disastrous, or institutional scripts that always put order above empathy.

When a student unravels, the bell rings, attendance is taken, lunch passes are clipped, and somewhere in an overworked office, a referral request percolates through a backlog stretching months, if not years. In the meantime, the child remains in class, awkwardly writhing in distress, as the system meticulously documents concern without ever finding the capacity to act.

This is not a failure of care. It is a failure of preparation.

Consider the average teacher-training syllabus. You'll find units on curriculum design, learning theories, and assessment strategies. But mental health? A single module, often optional, peppered with buzzwords: "resilience," "mindfulness," "CBT basics." No supervised clinical hours. No deep dives into trauma-informed pedagogy. No concrete guidelines for when a student's panic attack signals a deeper disorder.

One Ontario program advertised "two hours on student well-being," which boiled down to how to use a stress ball in class. A British Columbia college offered a "mental health in education" session that amounted to watching a documentary trailer and filling out a five-question quiz. Even when "mental health specialists" visit training cohorts, their instruction is framed around how to refer, not how to recognize or respond. Notice everything, understand nothing, keep the lesson plan intact.

Meanwhile, chronic resource shortages tighten like a vice. Class sizes climb, sometimes to forty or more, while budgets shrink in real terms. Special-education assistants are one per wing, counselling services are scarce, and when a student is flagged as a "special case," the unspoken reality is brutal: the school is neither staffed nor funded to handle it.

According to the Canadian Teachers' Federation, average class sizes have risen by 15 percent over the past decade, despite explicit policy targets to limit them. Per-pupil funding in many provinces has stagnated or dropped when adjusted for inflation. Administrative tasks, report cards, standardized tests, compliance paperwork, multiply, often commanding more attention than student support.

Students in distress face delays measured in lunar cycles. Psychological assessments typically take 6 months to 1 year to schedule. Once completed, referrals to child-and-adolescent mental health services encounter waitlists that rival emergency room corridors on a Friday night. During this time, the student is expected to sit in class, behave, and keep up academically, an impossible ask when anxiety, depression, or trauma is shaping every thought and movement.

In over ninety percent of Canadian schools, principals report a dire need for more mental health support. Yet fewer than ten percent have consistent access to a psychologist or clinical social worker. Counsellor-to-student ratios routinely exceed one professional for every 600 students, and in some rural or under-resourced urban schools, that ratio climbs past one to 1,000.

This is not an intervention; it is triage. A single counsellor trying to manage the compounding stress of hundreds of young minds means crisis prevention is a luxury, crisis response is firefighting, and chronic care is fiction. As one veteran counsellor in Manitoba said, “I’m at capacity before 9 a.m., and by 3 p.m. I’m just a referral factory. I see them, I write a note, I circle back next semester if anyone remembers.”

Amid this wasteland of support, teachers burn out. Emotional exhaustion, cynicism, and a sense of inefficacy are endemic. According to a 2022 pan-Canadian survey, 70 percent of educators report high stress levels related to student mental health concerns. Fifty-five percent exhibit signs of compassion fatigue. Thirty-eight percent have considered leaving the profession.

But here’s the kicker: instead of addressing causes, the response is to exhort teachers to “practice self-care” and “build resilience.” You’ll find workshops on yoga in the staffroom, newsletters on sleep hygiene, perhaps an online webinar on meditation for teachers, none of which addresses the fact that you can’t meditate away overcrowded classrooms or nonexistent referral pathways. There’s no structural change, only personal exhortation. Burnout becomes normalized; attrition accelerates; and the system, in turn, demands more resilience as if it were a renewable resource.

When mental health education does appear, it is often cosmetic. Mindfulness worksheets plaster the walls, a Zen doodle next to the periodic table. Resilience slogans: "Breathe in strength, breathe out fear." Hotline posters with numbers you call in a crisis that inevitably go to voicemail because nobody's on staff after 4 p.m.

Yes, awareness matters. Slogans can spark conversation. But when the only literacy students acquire is "mental illness is tragic and rare," the real lesson becomes "keep it hidden, or you will be cataloged as Other". Without depth, without genuine psychoeducation, mental illness remains an abstract concept. Students learn that depression is a sad meme and anxiety is something you "wish away." They do not learn that mental health issues are common, variable, and might very well be happening across the aisle.

Post-secondary institutions follow the same script but slap a heftier tuition bill on it. Well-endowed universities erect "integrated wellness hubs" with teletherapy platforms, 24/7 hotlines, and drop-in clinics. Underfunded colleges ration five free sessions per student per academic year. Rural campuses have... nothing. The equity gap widens according to postal code and bank balance.

Data from the Canadian Association of College and University Student Services shows that on some campuses, waitlists for on-campus counsellors exceed six weeks. In contrast, private teletherapy can charge $150 per session, well beyond most student budgets. So, wellness becomes a privilege, not a right.

The statistics are grim, but no one is surprised. Anxiety and depression rates among post-secondary students hover above forty percent. Suicide is the second leading cause of death for those aged 15–24. Dropout rates climb. Academic accommodations, extensions, and reduced course loads are inconsistently applied or subject to invasive documentation requirements. Still, institutions feign astonishment when pressure yields collapse.

Paradoxically, we have blueprints for success.

• School-based mental health literacy programs in Australia saw a 30 percent increase in early help-seeking behaviours.

• Trauma-informed teacher training in select U.S. districts cut disciplinary referrals by 40 percent.
• Integrated support, where psychologists, social workers, and educators co-locate, reduces crisis escalations by half.
• Peer-support initiatives in Ontario increased student engagement metrics by 20 percent and halved waitlists.
• Housing First experiments demonstrate that stable living conditions for homeless youth improve school attendance by 60 percent.

The evidence is overwhelming. Dollars invested in mental health infrastructure yield clear educational dividends: fewer dropouts, reduced disciplinary incidents, improved academic performance, lower crisis referrals, and healthier communities. Someone should point this out to the powers that be.

The policies are in place, on paper. In theory, students have the right to accommodation; in practice, they navigate a labyrinth of forms, waitlists, and "we'll get back to you" apologies. Teachers are told they're vital, essential, heroes, and then left alone in overcrowded classrooms to catch the fragments of children slipping through the cracks.

The invisible straitjacket that binds students and educators is not accidental. It is a policy made quietly. Budgets are pegged to outdated formulas. Staffing ratios are suggested, not enforced. Mental health is an add-on line item, not the foundation upon which schooling rests.

Until education systems treat mental health as infrastructure rather than optional décor, they will continue to notice suffering, document it thoroughly, and pass it along until someone else takes the hit.

The cost is measured not only in teacher burnout and student dropouts, but in long-term unemployment, chronic housing instability, and cycles of marginalization that echo across generations. Schools proudly proclaim that they prepare students for the real world. In this, at least, they succeed, because the real world doesn't pause to rescue the wounded either.

Chapter Ten
The Criminal Justice System as a Modern Asylum

If Chapter Four forced you to recoil at the cold precision of courts, cells, and sentences, tighten your belt; this ride only accelerates into even darker corridors. We detoured through education, housing, work, and stigma to reveal how society rigs the deck against mental health long before a defendant ever faces a judge. Without that backdrop, the cruelty inside looks like chaos; with it, it's a greased machine humming behind steel doors and buzzing intercoms. Now we must stare unflinchingly at the truth: our prisons, jails, and courts have become default mental institutions, where compassion is elective, red tape is the corset, and outdated policy clamps down as ruthlessly as any straitjacket ever did. The padded rooms and rigid routines live on in modern garb, but now the patients shuffle through buzzing courtrooms, fluorescent-lit probation offices, and clanging cellblocks, trapped in a cycle designed not to heal but only to contain.

Sanity assessments, legally cloaked as the insanity defence, are our grim gateway into this maze. At its heart, this defence claims that because of a mental disease or defect at the moment of the crime, the accused lacked mens rea, the criminal "guilty mind." But the tests, M'Naghten's understanding-of-wrongfulness standard, the irresistible-impulse test, vary by jurisdiction, cloaked in jargon that mystifies defendants, lawyers, and the public alike. In the U.S., M'Naghten and irresistible impulse remain the hallmarks; Canada's "not criminally responsible on account of mental disorder" mirrors M'Naghten but pledges a delicate balance between safety and genuine treatment. Pedants note that the 1843 House of Lords' M'Naghten rule, sometimes spelled McNaughton, still governs insanity defences across the U.K., U.S., and Canada, a testament to legal inertia in the face of evolving science. This labyrinth of precedent and policy burdens defendants with arcane criteria, often without clear guidance or hope of understanding it.

At this volatile intersection of law and illness stand forensic psychiatrists, forced to translate humanity's messiest realities into checkbox logic and crisp reports. Their verdict can shunt a person toward punishment or toward treatment, or, more often, slap them with a hybrid of both. Hollywood's courtroom fireworks aside, insanity pleas are scarce and successes rarer still. Yet this defence is no stage prop. It remains our last line of defence against punishing those whose minds have betrayed them, a desperate reminder that law and care are perilously intertwined and all too often torn apart by budget caps, bureaucracy, and stigma.

Beyond innocence or guilt, these same psychiatrists shape sentencing and risk assessments that echo through parole hearings and future-release decisions. Courts, desperate for reliable guidance, lean on their expertise to sketch out rehabilitation plans, correctional program assignments, and future-risk forecasts. In theory, this ensures decisions factor in mental health; in practice, that noble ideal drowns beneath systemic inertia, where reports languish in files and recommendations gather dust on shelves.

Traditional incarceration has a shameful legacy of aggravating mental distress. Jails become echo chambers of despair, where the clang of doors and harsh lights intensify anxiety and paranoia. So Mental Health Courts and diversion programs have emerged like fractured lifelines. These specialized courts flip the script: judges moonlight as therapists, probation officers as case managers, and defence attorneys as uneasy hybrids of advocate and overseer. Success is redefined, fewer guilty verdicts, fewer stifling sentences, more sustained symptom management and community reintegration. Participants follow tailor-made regimens of medication management, individual and group therapy, substance counselling, housing aid, job training, and nonstop case management. The payoff is real: slashed re-arrest rates, shorter stays behind bars, brighter minds, and slightly less overcrowded facilities. The irony, however, continues to glare; our justice system, once a de facto asylum of neglect, now pretends at therapy.

Yet the metaphorical corset remains as tight as ever: scarce resources, patchy access, endless bureaucracy. Remember, the old asylum never closed; in this instance, it just traded padded cells for piles of paperwork.

Diversion programs intercept suspects before prosecution, promising care instead of charges and, hopefully, release instead of lasting arrest records, if only a robust network of community services exists to catch them. Without outpatient therapy slots, 24/7 crisis teams, supportive housing vacancies, and vocational support, diversion collapses into a slapdash bandage over a gaping wound, leaving vulnerable people bouncing back into courts and cages.

For those who slip past diversions, the punishment cells await. Prisons aren't clinics; they're bleak factories of compliance. Cramped quarters, no privacy, months-long waiting lists for psychiatric assessment, and almost no dedicated mental health professionals collaborate to form a toxic stew. High staff turnover and undertrained corrections officers only deepen disorders, turning incarceration into a modern asylum where the straitjacket is bureaucratic neglect, verbal abuse, and isolation. Literally back to square one.

Inside these walls, the spectrum of suffering is staggering, from mild depression and post-traumatic stress to full-blown schizophrenia and manic bipolar swings, topped by self-harm incidents and suicide attempts that tragically spike in intake units. Add addiction and withdrawal to the mix, and maintaining any semblance of treatment feels like juggling chainsaws over a pit of spikes.

Ideally, prisons would staff psychiatrists, psychologists, social workers, and counsellors; screen every entrant on intake; run tiered care from crisis intervention to intensive therapy; preserve treatment across transfers and releases; tie mental health to vocational and educational programming; and train guards to de-escalate rather than brutalize. But containment remains the core mission, so care is relegated to an afterthought. The result: a red-taped asylum where the straitjacket is indifference, chronic underfunding, and institutional inertia.

Criminalizing mental illness isn't a bug; it's a feature. Loitering ordinances, public intoxication rules, and disorderly-conduct statutes loop people through courts and cells without ever addressing the underlying illness. Institutions built for care can't deliver it, guaranteeing that punishment remains the default response to behaviours born of untreated conditions.

Here, forensic psychiatry should bridge clinical truth and legal need: competency evaluations, housing and treatment recommendations, risk mitigation strategies. Instead, we have reality: understaffing leaves detainees in limbo, waiting months for court-ordered assessments that sometimes never materialize.

Yes, the U.S. Eighth Amendment and Canada's Charter of Rights and Freedoms demand adequate care, but the chasm between constitutional promises and on-the-ground practice yawns wide, sustained by underinvestment and impossible logistics. The system dangles treatment like a carrot on a stick; the reward is delay, neglect, and the chilling message that mental illness here is itself criminal.

This modern asylum stands as a blistering indictment of societal failure. When community mental health cracks, jails become orphanages of untreated illness, often to devastating ends. Many enter for petty offences and emerge more traumatized, alienated from health and hope, ensnared in a vicious cycle of crime and illness feeding one another. The remedy is clear but rarely embraced: invest upstream in community services, expand diversion programs and Mental Health Courts, and commit to genuine rehabilitation for those behind bars.

Reforming prison mental health is more than ticking a legal box; it's an ethical imperative and public safety necessity. Treatment inside must mirror community standards: proper staffing ratios, real psychiatric and psychological services, thorough medication management, and a full suite of cognitive, behavioural, and group therapies. Guards must learn empathy, de-escalation techniques, and to view mental illness as medical, not moral. Peer-support programs and inmate mental health councils can further humanize the process. Until these become standard, the modern asylum label remains all too literal.

Equally urgent is broadening alternatives to incarceration for nonviolent offences born of mental illness. Punishing symptoms as crimes erects a revolving door of arrest and release. Diversion, crisis-intervention teams, and Therapeutic Community Courts offer a path out, address the condition, not merely its outburst. Imagine someone in a psychotic break steered into care, not a cell, their record cleared, and real hope restored.

These solutions hinge on robust community services: outpatient clinics, mobile crisis teams, supported housing, vocational training, and seamless transitions between systems. They're lifelines, not luxuries. Justice for those with mental illness can't stop at courtroom exits or prison gates; it must follow into communities, focusing on recovery, reintegration, and true public safety. Anything less props up the modern asylum, swaddled in legal rhetoric and institutional indifference.

Consider the numbers: 15–20 percent of U.S. jail inmates and 10–15 percent of state prisoners have serious mental illness; Canada sits around 17 percent. If incarceration cured anything, these figures wouldn't hover so stubbornly high. Mental Health Courts cut recidivism by 20–35 percent in the U.S. and 25–30 percent in Canada. Yet only 5–10 percent of eligible

U.S. offenders and 10–15 percent in Canada ever access diversion, a slender fraction of those who need it. Psychiatric wait times behind bars stretch two to six months in the U.S. and one to three months in Canada.

Financially, each Mental Health Court participant saves $10,000–15,000 a year in the U.S., $8,000–12,000 in Canada, underscoring that humane justice is also cost-effective. Still, only 30–40 percent of U.S. and 35–45 percent of Canadian facilities offer meaningful re-entry programs. Most inmates face the chasm alone, with budget shortfalls spiralling as needs grow.

These figures confirm what we dread: the modern asylum thrives. It's donned correctional blues instead of stripes, but its grip is iron. Some states and provinces experiment with fixes, crisis diversion teams, court liaisons, and community treatment mandates, yet the gaps remain wide, the stakes are sky-high, and the human, social, and financial tolls are staggering.

Confinement extends beyond justice; it wears a white coat, too. In Canada and the U.S., police and doctors can detain those deemed dangerous for emergency or extended involuntary hospitalization, laws pitched as protective bulwarks but routinely functioning as bureaucratic straitjackets. Civil rights and dignity are meant to temper this power, yet history teaches us that the scales rarely balance, and vulnerable people can languish for weeks or months without proper treatment.

Quebec's Mental Health Act codifies three tiers of involuntary hospitalization:

1. Preventive Confinement (72-hour hold), an emergency lifeline or blunt instrument, decided by a physician or nurse practitioner, with only basic rights notification.
2. Temporary Confinement (up to 144 hours), a court-involved process requiring two psychiatric assessments before bedlam meets bureaucracy.
3. Court-Authorized Confinement, indefinite detention reviewed every 21 days and then every three months, a revolving door of oversight that juggles paternalism against personal liberty.

These legal structures promise protection and accountability, but often deliver overreach and prolonged detention without genuine therapeutic intervention. Coercive treatment under the banner of "public safety" masks containment as care. Transparency and oversight strive to restrain abuse but battle a system that too readily substitutes supervision for true healing.

Perhaps a bit of elaboration is required. Québec's Mental Health Act is a prime example of the delicate balance between Protection and Rights.

Québec's *Loi sur la protection des personnes*, more commonly known as P-38.001, is the legal mechanism that determines when the province may temporarily deprive a person of their freedom "for their own good". It governs when someone can be taken to a hospital and confined without consent because their mental state is deemed dangerous. The intent is officially protective, benevolent even, yet the lived reality often feels less like care and more like a velvet-gloved seizure of autonomy. It is the law that assures the public it is saving lives, while quietly reminding individuals that liberty is conditional, fragile, and revocable on short notice. The concept is good; the applications... not always.

The law operates through three principal mechanisms (a rough breakdown of who and under what circumstances the laws and time periods mentioned earlier may be enforced):

• **Preventive confinement of up to 72 hours**, where a physician may order psychiatric observation without a court order if the individual's mental state appears to pose a grave and immediate danger, a determination often made quickly, conservatively, and with institutional liability firmly in mind.

• **Police intervention**, where officers may transport a person to a hospital against their will when they have serious reason to believe a danger exists, frequently following a 911 call or a request from a crisis worker or concerned third party, and rarely accompanied by nuance.

• **Court-ordered psychiatric evaluation and confinement**, used when danger is alleged but not immediate, allowing the legal system to formalize what has already begun, with psychiatric examinations serving as both medical assessment and bureaucratic justification.

In practice, police involvement is the most visible and psychologically jarring gateway into the P-38 process. When officers arrive, they are not there to mediate, contextualize, or untangle the emotional archaeology of a situation. They are there to act. Once danger is alleged, discretion evaporates. Compliance becomes mandatory. The individual is escorted, restrained if necessary, and transported. The uniform may say "police," not "corrections," but the experience registers the same in the nervous system. The destination may be a hospital rather than a jail, yet the body does not care about semantics when it is being escorted by force.

To be clear, the benefits of this system are not theoretical. P-38 has saved lives. When someone is actively suicidal, floridly psychotic, violently disorganized, or profoundly detached from reality, involuntary intervention can interrupt tragedy. People who are incapable of recognizing their own deterioration are sometimes stabilized, treated, and returned to the world with resources they would never have accepted voluntarily. In justice-related contexts, the Act allows individuals whose crimes are entangled with severe mental illness to be diverted from standard incarceration into psychiatric facilities, where the goal is treatment rather than punishment, or at least a more civilized approximation of it.

And yet, this same system carries a shadow long enough to eclipse its good intentions. P-38 is an exceptional legal regime precisely because it suspends fundamental rights. Liberty, autonomy, and bodily self-determination are paused based on perceived risk, assessed rapidly, often conservatively, and almost always upstream of meaningful judicial oversight. Safeguards exist, yes, but they arrive after the doors have already locked. By the time rights are explained, the person has already been deprived of them.

The most contentious feature of the Act is not the confinement itself, but the ease with which the machinery can be set in motion. While crisis workers are the preferred gatekeepers, reality is messier. Spouses, partners, and family members can and do initiate police involvement, particularly in moments of emotional chaos. In cases of domestic abuse or coercive control, this becomes especially dangerous. Advocacy groups and legal observers have raised concerns about instances where P-38 has been used as a weapon rather than a safeguard. A false or exaggerated claim, once filtered through police protocol, can result in forced hospitalization with little immediate recourse for the person on the receiving end.

Even when abuse is not present, ordinary human conflict can become the spark. Arguments escalate. Emotions flare. Someone says something reckless, despairing, or angry. Someone else decides it sounds dangerous enough to call for help. At that point, the situation no longer belongs to either party. It belongs to the system. Police arrive. Tension hardens into procedure. What might have been a bad night becomes a psychiatric record. What might have been an argument becomes an institutional memory. The individual taken may emerge days later stabilized, yes, but also humiliated, distrustful, and quietly altered.

These ethical fractures are not unique to Québec. The United Kingdom's Mental Health Act offers a parallel cautionary tale, particularly under Sections 2 and 3, which authorize detention for assessment and treatment, respectively. Like P-38, UK sectioning relies on risk-based judgments and often involves police assistance. Like P-38, it has been criticized for overreach, inequitable application, and the psychological harm inflicted by involuntary detention. Across jurisdictions, the language changes. The experience does not.

Further complicating matters is the distinction between confinement and treatment. Under Québec law, being detained does not automatically authorize treatment without consent. Separate legal steps are required, creating a surreal limbo where a person may be held for their safety but denied agency over what happens to their body and mind. The result is a system that can feel less like care and more like containment, reinforcing the perception that the primary goal is control rather than healing.

P-38.001 ultimately exists in a moral gray zone that the law pretends is black and white. It is indispensable in true crises and deeply harmful when misapplied. It can rescue people from the brink and simultaneously teach them that seeking help is dangerous. It reassures the public while quietly eroding trust among those most likely to need care again.

As with the UK's sectioning laws, provincial and state laws across Canada and the US, the unresolved challenge is not whether involuntary intervention should exist, but how often, how easily, and at whose expense it is deployed. Without relentless scrutiny, trauma-informed practice, and an honest acknowledgment of power imbalance, a law designed to save lives risks becoming another chapter in why so many people learn to fear the very systems meant to protect them.

The ultimate challenge is ensuring legal power doesn't become another straitjacket. Whether in hospitals, courts, or prisons, interventions must heal and protect, not merely contain. Strengthening independent oversight boards, bulking up community resources, and weaving specialized legal corridors are crucial if we're serious about stopping hospitals, courts, and prisons from playing interchangeable jailers.

In the end, the justice system mirrors our collective failure to care for mental illness. Yes, prisons and courts echo old asylums, but they also spotlight paths to reform. Choosing rehabilitation over punishment, treatment instead of containment, and humanity rather than indifference should always be the priority. The straitjacket has morphed into legislation and red tape. So, do we decide to let it tighten further or finally loosen its hold and forge a system where justice and care truly coexist?

Chapter Eleven
Current State of "Care"

From the 1950s until now, mental health "reform" in Canada and the United States has been less a straight line of progress and more a series of tectonic shifts crashing into human lives. Enormous psychiatric institutions, pillars of brick, steel bars, and padded cells, were shuttered; thousands of beds vanished. A minority of rooms reappeared in general-hospital psychiatric wings, while a patchwork of community programs and private group homes tried (and mostly failed) to catch the people cut loose. Outwardly, the crumbling asylums have disappeared; inside, the same forces of confinement, crisis, and bureaucratic oversight haunt living rooms, emergency wards, and the souls of patients and families. To trace this grim evolution, we begin in Canada, then we'll bleed southward into the United States

In the early 1960s, provincial mental hospitals were Canada's safety net for people living with severe psychiatric illness. Then, in just fifteen years, roughly 35,000 of those beds were slashed. By 1975, only about 15,000 hospital beds remained, while general hospitals grudgingly added some 5,000 psychiatric spots, far less than the disappearing asylum capacity. Overnight, thousands of patients were sent home with nothing but a lion's share of warning: a hastily written discharge summary and a prescription.

The cold statistics, often quoted in Ontario Human Rights Commission reports, are stark yet incomplete. They chronicle the demolition of institutions, not the collapse of human lives. Discharged patients roamed cities in search of help that wasn't there.

Siblings and parents juggled phone calls to overwhelmed crisis helplines, pleaded with underfunded clinics, begged pharmacists for more time on essential medication. Some ended up in emergency rooms, only to be released hours later with a pill bottle tucked into their coat and a phone number they had already tried. Others never called for help at all, stranded in apartments that became isolation cells. The system toppling in on itself left a generation of mentally ill people and their families navigating a labyrinth with no minotaur to fight, only mirrors reflecting their own desperation.

When politicians declared "care" shifted into the community, they handed you a map dotted with new clinics and group homes. But counting roofs in a landscape suffering a drought of resources is like tallying umbrellas when the sky hasn't opened in months. A more revealing measure is beds per capita and real spending devoted to mental health.

In 1959, Canada boasted robust psychiatric capacity: hundreds of beds per 100,000 people, enough to treat, stabilize, and sometimes cure. Today, even considering general-hospital beds and private residential facilities, the ratio has plunged into the low tens per 100,000. The mid-century architecture that once cradled patients has been largely dismantled, as if outpatient programs could magically absorb every crisis, every psychotic break, every family fraying at the seams.

And the money, or the pretense of it, ramps up the irony. Between 2000 and 2020, total health expenditures tripled from roughly $100 billion to $300 billion. Hospitals gobble up about a quarter of that bounty, yet psychiatric beds remain scarce, and community investments tick upward just enough to flash a headline-friendly commitment. The result isn't better care but a frenzy of bureaucracy: committees meet, reports multiply, families and patients shoulder the fallout. Crowded hospital wards spill into hallways; community programs buckle under waitlists; the individual's fate depends on the luck of which social worker has an opening, who picks up the phone first, or whether a neighbour takes pity on a panicked late-night knock.

CIHI data reveals a stark shift: Canadians aged 65 and older accounted for 44.7 percent of health-care dollars in 2012, rising to 46.9 percent by 2022 and into 2024. Long-term care homes, continuing care, and home-care services for seniors swallow up resources, while mental-health programs, scattered among hospitals, physician billings, community initiatives, and tiny social-service grants, fight over whatever crumbs remain. Every dollar poured into subacute senior care is a dollar not spent on crisis teams, outpatient counselling, night-line staff, or psychosocial rehabilitation for people with acute psychosis. It's a political math trick that promises universal compassion for visibly frail seniors and leaves people with severe mental illness in the shadows. The elderly win the spotlight, the votes, and the funding; mental-health patients are left to balance on a seesaw rigged against them.

Despite endless white papers, roundtable conferences, and glossy "mental-health strategy" press releases, Canada still falls far short. The 2024 State of Mental Health in Canada report shows that provinces allocate an average of just 6.3 percent of their health budgets to mental health, barely half the 12 percent recommended by global experts. Meanwhile, elder care soaks up nearly half the pie, keeping their provincial average at 46.9 percent. Political headlines promise expanded access; budgets inch forward by token amounts. The enduring result: patients, families, and underpaid front-line workers bear the weight of a system that dangles hope while hoarding resources.

This chronic underinvestment fuels a crisis of despair. About 2.5 million Canadians with mental-health needs report inadequate care, a population roughly the size of Manitoba plus Saskatchewan. Self-rated mental health is plummeting; in 2019, only 8.9

percent of Canadians described their mental health as "poor" or "fair." By 2021, that figure leapt to 26 percent. In three short years, the percentage of people floundering emotionally tripled, leaping far beyond anything policy wonks predicted or prepared for.

Not everyone is dragged down equally. Indigenous Peoples bear disproportionate burdens: 38 percent report their mental health as "poor" or "fair," a symptom of intergenerational trauma, systemic neglect, and cultural dislocation. Young adults, too, especially those aged 18 to 24, face a Kafkaesque maze: 57 percent identify resource scarcity as a barrier to care.

Socioeconomic fallout follows predictably: fewer than half of Canadians with mental-health disabilities hold employment, while the rest rely on income supports that often keep them mired in poverty, which only exacerbates their condition. Struggling to pay rent or afford a prescription becomes a full-time job, further cementing the cycle of mental illness and material deprivation.

Even data collection, crucial for planning, has become a casualty of this neglect. Without comprehensive, consistent information on service availability, wait times, and patient outcomes, policymakers rely on stale assumptions and luck. Psychiatric facilities remain frozen in time, lacking sensory rooms or quiet spaces that could defuse a crisis. Instead, staff resort to restrictive interventions, restraints, seclusion/isolation rooms, and emergency sedation, as if restraining people were a solution rather than a symptom of resource failure. Stitch all these fractures together, and you see a system incapable of meeting growing needs, a machine that calls itself "care" while shrugging at its own cruelty.

Crossing the border, you encounter a similar horror. In the U.S., surveys estimate that 23–24 percent of adults, over 60 million people, experienced mental illness in the past year, and 5.6 percent faced a serious mental illness. Keep in mind that Canada's population is roughly 40 million people, and it is the second-largest country in the world. Those suffering mental illness in the US could double the population of Canada......The highest prevalence is among 18-to-

25-year-olds, a cohort promised the dawn of independence yet grappling with anxiety, depression, and trauma at unprecedented rates.

Access? A wall. NAMI reports that only 50.6 percent of those with any mental illness received treatment in the past year. Half of all adults with diagnosable conditions, mothers, fathers, veterans, and retail workers receive no help at all. Men, certain racial and ethnic minorities, and people in rural areas are even less likely to make it through the labyrinth. About 70.8 percent of those with serious mental illness get some treatment, but tens of millions remain without consistent support, left to fend for themselves or risk destitution.

Inpatient psychiatric beds in the U.S. number roughly 28.4 per 100,000 people, well below expert estimates of 40–60 per 100,000 needed to meet demand. Total capacity hovers between 113,000 and 134,000 beds, most of which are in private psychiatric hospitals. Public and non-profit facilities hold a thinner slice: about 36,000 adult beds in state hospitals, just 10.8 per 100,000. No federal mandate sets a minimum. States scramble to meet historical norms and comparative benchmarks, but many fall short of even the barest threshold.

The result is carnage in emergency departments. Patients linger in hallways for days, sometimes weeks. Involuntary-commitment orders pile up in court dockets as judges and physicians debate who truly qualifies for the few beds available. Meanwhile, people in crisis end up in jails, homeless encampments, or worse, dead by suicide because no bed was free when they needed it most.

Even where patients slip through the cracks of denial and enter care, the conditions within often resemble the institutions we supposedly abandoned. Ward wings with peeling paint, broken windows, understaffed shifts, and treatment models that hark back to containment-first philosophies: lock the door, sedate the patient, transfer liability. The loudspeaker blares a page for staff to a code in Room 12, yet no one comes quickly because there simply aren't enough workers. Quiet rooms, sensory corners, and trauma-informed spaces are luxuries. Overmedication and chemical restraints persist as if progress were a myth.

So here we stand, mental illness is pervasive on both sides of the border. Suffering climbs exponentially. Yet the promises of reform, deinstitutionalization, community care, and parity of esteem have delivered an experience that is, at best, patchy and, at worst, catastrophic. Survey data and budget figures can obscure these stories, but for those who enter the system, the real test begins the moment they step through the door. Will they find a compassionate, responsive team with time, space, and resources to help them heal? Or will they encounter a skeleton crew, empty rooms, and a waiting line that stretches toward oblivion?

To grasp today's mental-health system, we must nudge aside the comforting rhetoric of progress and peer into the rubble we've built. Dunked in policy jargon, this is not care. It's a grim charade that forces patients, families, and front-line workers to perform miracles on a shoestring, while bureaucrats applaud from a safe distance. So, we're at the current state of "care": a fractured, underfunded, overcrowded maze where survival depends on luck, grit, and the kindness of strangers.

Chapter Twelve
The Human Cost of Mental Health Hospitalization

Statistics can chart every vacancy and every stretched-thin clinician, yet they fail to show the soul of hospitalization today: crumbling walls, barren hallways, and an overreliance on isolation and restraint that treats human beings like hazards to be contained. Chronic underinvestment isn't an accounting footnote; it's a punitive architecture that shapes patient identity, reinforcing trauma instead of relieving it.

Chronic staff shortages poison every corner of psychiatric facilities. When there aren't enough psychiatrists, psychologists, or specially trained nurses, care becomes reactive firefighting rather than a therapeutic partnership. Time meant for nuanced assessment and de-escalation is swallowed up by constant crisis management. As human connection withers, cold physical space steps in hallways masquerading as group rooms, locked doors stand in for conversation, and isolation rooms graduate from "rare emergency tool" to "institutional necessity."

In the U.S., fewer than one-third of people live in areas with enough psychiatrists to meet local needs, and more than half of the counties have none at all. Canada's universal-healthcare mantle offers some protection, but decades of underfunding mean patients still face long waits and subpar conditions. The scarcity of beds, aging facilities, and barren therapeutic environments does more than limit comfort; they actively sabotage recovery.

Step into an unrenovated psychiatric unit that still smells faintly of the Cold War, and you'll see it: crowded, fluorescent corridors with minimal privacy and zero quiet or sensory space. Harsh lights glare off hard floors. Anxiety, agitation, and boredom echo down hallways. Patients who try to engage in therapy are waging war on the very design of their surroundings, an environment crafted to frustrate emotional regulation rather than support it.

Overcrowding and punishingly low staff-to-patient ratios make individual attention a mythical luxury. Clinicians, stretched nearly to breaking, default to coercion, seclusion, physical restraints, forced medication, because there simply isn't time or space for gentler, voluntary de-escalation. Emergency measures become regular procedure, eroding trust and distributing trauma. Patients bounce between stabilization and relapse in spaces that neither soothe nor empower, forging the very institutional dependency society claims to despise.

Access to therapy, recreational programs, or meaningful social interaction is often a rumour rather than a reality. In both Canada and the U.S., these mental-health facilities do more than inconvenience; they worsen psychological distress, prolong hospitalizations, and perpetuate relapse cycles. The great irony: decades of shuttering beds under the banner of modernization, only to trap patients in ever-prettier waiting rooms for misery.

Despite it all, even in America's bleak landscape, there are pockets of promise. At Jackson Behavioural Health in Florida and in some select New York State psychiatric units, trauma-informed design, comfort rooms, sensory spaces, and layouts built for voluntary regulation have slashed reliance on seclusion and restraint. Patients allowed to self-soothe spend less time admitted, exhibit lower agitation levels, and relapse less often. The contrast with most Canadian wards could not be starker: endless hallways, buzzing fluorescents, and seats bolted to the floor; no quiet rooms, no sensory retreats, just overstimulation, stress, and unrelenting frustration.

Research is ruthless in its clarity: environments that let patients choose de-escalation dramatically improve outcomes. Those who force control actively exacerbate harm, driving higher relapse rates and hindering community reintegration. Recovery is not dictated by medication charts alone; it is woven into the dignity of the spaces where care unfolds. Pinel and Tuke, pioneers of humane treatment, understood that painful truth more than two centuries ago. By their measure, decades-old infrastructure and chronic neglect aren't abstract policy failures; they are concrete engines of suffering.

Canada's mental-health infrastructure reads like a history of misplaced priorities. Patients are funnelled into wards built for broken bones and pneumonia, enduring overcrowded rooms, harsh décor, and glaring voids where therapeutic spaces should be. Meanwhile, abundant evidence from U.S. pilots shows that natural light, acoustic dampening, private nooks, and outdoor access shorten stays, boost therapy engagement, and reduce relapse. Canada's adoption of these elements has been sporadic, token, and insufficient. Without serious investment in patient-centred design, equitable bed distribution, and transparent reporting, Canadian patients remain trapped on a never-ending carousel of crisis and readmission.

Both countries share a tragedy-induced comedic symmetry: mid-century bed closures, from roughly hundreds per 100,000 residents to a "historic low" of 10–15 in the U.S., have forced people in acute crisis into ER hallways, city streets, or jail cells, because those are the only beds left. In Canada, the loss of roughly 35,000 psychiatric beds between 1960 and 1975 never spurred trauma-informed rebuilding; instead, psychiatric wings were grafted onto general hospitals with layouts designed for X-rays, not emotional crises.

Hôtel-Dieu de Sherbrooke stands as a stark emblem. Its original pavilions were built from 1939 to

1943 as a tuberculosis sanatorium. The 1971 addition of the Pavillon Émile Noël now houses the region's psychiatric wards and follows the same outdated cell-block logic: long corridors, rooms aligned like prison cells, shared bathrooms, and nursing stations that double as command centers. Isolation rooms stare at staff hubs like tiny surveillance pods. Communal spaces are token at best; opportunities for privacy are virtually nonexistent unless you manage to hide in one of two small gender-neutral shared bathrooms found on each floor. That is, until staff eventually notice you aren't in your room or prowling the hall. Televisions and phones are communal property, and most residents sleep in rooms with two to four patients each. Only a select few secure one of the handful of allotted single rooms, a respite usually granted only to institutional veterans, the majority of whom are elderly. Of the multiple wards spanning several floors, the one that differs is the seventh-floor forensic psychiatric wing, which favours security over comfort, as if design alone can contain danger.

The predictable outcome is heartbreak. Patients pace overstimulated corridors, stare vacantly out windows, or huddle in rooms that offer no solace. Visitation is restricted to public, staff-monitored areas, stripping away any chance of privacy or family intimacy. Every sound reverberates; there is no refuge from noise except the brief reprieve of lights-out confinement at night. If the patients cooperate and go to sleep.

Across Canada, the story repeats. Deinstitutionalization closed tens of thousands of beds, but instead of building modern, trauma-informed facilities, services were shoehorned into repurposed hospital wings. Corridors meant for X-ray transfers now magnify pacing and agitation; nursing stations double as control towers; rooms intended for post-op rest become de facto cells. Trauma-sensitive design is often no more than a bullet point in policy manuals or an occasional pilot study. The majority of patients deal with wards that are nothing more than preserved artifacts, unfit for modern psychiatric care.

This neglect comes at a human cost. Community-based supports may have grown on spreadsheets, but inpatient capacity and quality have not. Patients are admitted to wings built for surgery and cancer patients, and outpatient follow-up is a precarious patchwork. True recovery demands more than medication and sporadic therapy; it requires spaces that facilitate dignity, autonomy, and self-regulation.

Evidence is indisputable: sightlines that let staff monitor without hovering, quiet rooms, natural light, acoustic absorption and control, along with outdoor therapeutic areas, reduce the need for coercive measures, cut conflict incidents, shorten stays, and elevate patient and staff satisfaction. Chaotic, overcrowded, noisy wards accelerate agitation, disrupt sleep, and drive staff burnout.

Nurses describe caring in these settings as "walking through history rather than managing a crisis." Paperwork devours hours that should be spent in human connection. Outdated infrastructure and the lack of voluntary de-escalation spaces transform fatigue into coercion. In under-resourced wards, restraint, seclusion, and forced medication spike, not from malevolence, but from the absence of any safer alternatives.

The consequences extend far beyond hospital walls. Discharged patients, unmoored by chaotic hospitalization, return to communities with fractured outpatient systems. The revolving door spins faster, symptoms worsen, emergency services overflow, and relapses multiply. Staff, worn thin and disillusioned, quit in alarming numbers, leaving the system propped up only by extraordinary personal resilience, leaving an unsustainable, unjust model.

In the U.S., the collapse of state psychiatric beds has been truly catastrophic: mid-century peaks of hundreds per 100,000 residents plummeted to today's 10–15. Acute crises end up in ER hallways and jail cells because no beds remain. The architecture, aging, sterile, and overcrowded, bears witness to decades of policy failure. Even the best modern design flounders without adequate staffing: quiet rooms are useless if no one can supervise them; natural light is meaningless if admission takes days.

Patients endure fluorescent-lit gauntlets, buzzing alarms, crowded corridors, and minimal privacy. Physical and chemical restraints, forced medication, and cancelled recreational activities amplify trauma. Patients leave not just with diagnoses, but with psychological souvenirs of spaces that punished them for being unwell.

Psychiatric hospitalization has become a high-stakes gamble: brief stabilization shadowed by environmental trauma. Short stays, high readmission rates, and chronic understaffing make true recovery fleeting. Across Canada and the U.S., hospitalization treads the line between care and constraint. Overcrowded wards, retrofitted spaces, and exhausted staff are universal for both countries. Both systems tout modern therapies that environments hostile to healing actively undermine.

In the U.S., shorter stays coincide with climbing readmissions, ranging from roughly 7% in the best systems to 15% in the worst, a testament to system dysfunction, not patient failure. In Canada, universal coverage softens the blow, but overcrowding, antiquated facilities, and scant community support keep patients on an exhausting cycle of crisis and readmission.

Combined, North America's psychiatric hospitalization narrative is harrowing: a promised lifeline that often doubles as a source of fresh trauma. Patients confront seclusion rooms, restraints, forced medication, and sparse therapeutic space. Chronic understaffing, overcrowding, and inequitable access amplify harm. Without reform, hospitalization will remain a wearying cycle rather than a genuine path to recovery.

Stopping the revolving door will not and cannot happen overnight; it requires a careful evaluation and renovation of the system, and the system demands four interconnected reforms:

1. Inpatient Capacity: Beds are the foundation. Without them, crises can't be stabilized, and the revolving door spins on.
2. Staffing: Even the most thoughtful design is futile without enough clinicians, nurses, and support staff to monitor, guide therapy, and intervene early.
3. Community Supports: Housing, peer networks, social services, and robust outpatient care are essential. Discharge planning without follow-up is no

care at all.
4. Physical Environment: Evidence underlines the power of quiet rooms, sensory spaces, natural light, and outdoor areas to reduce coercion, bolster emotional regulation, and accelerate recovery.

Beds, personnel, community supports, and environments must align. Until they do, psychiatric hospitalization in North America will continue to test endurance rather than deliver genuine care.

Chapter Thirteen
The Language of Pathology and Its Social Implications

From Pinel's early humane reforms to today's DSM-5 thrill ride, translating raw human anguish into neat categories has been an epic, ongoing farce. Enter the DSM, the Diagnostic and Statistical Manual of Mental Disorders, the Holy Tablet for psychiatric obsessives, policy bureaucrats, and anyone willing to endure three hours of pedantic debate over whether a symptom cluster merits "mild," "moderate," or "spectacularly catastrophic" status. For decades, it's attempted the impossible: corralling grief, rage, confusion, and existential dread into checkboxes. Without it, describing your depression might look less like a conversation and more like a charade's routine performed by eight flailing octopuses. Try staging your quiet office-bathroom meltdown without someone popping their head in to argue whether it qualifies as a single or recurrent Major Depressive Episode. Yeah....Good luck.

These labels are far from academic busywork; they steer the entire care machine. They decide what treatments you can get, which services open their doors, and, crucially in the U.S., which claims insurers grudgingly foot. Labels equal power. But wielding that power exacts a cost: in flattening the mess of real lives into symptom lists, nuance is sacrificed. Humans are not textbooks. Symptoms overlap. Context matters. A diagnosis is a one-size-fits-all cap: it covers the noggin, but it itches, restricts, and sometimes tilts your ears outward in embarrassing ways, yet everyone insists it fits.

Then comes the social circus of labelling. Once you're stamped "diagnosed," the world has carte blanche to judge you. A diagnosis can be liberating, validating your pain, directing you to care, answering the nagging question: Am I broken or is this life? It can unlock peer support and peer-validated roadmaps from despair, a flashlight in the dark tunnel of distress if you really want to bank in metaphors. But labels also become social duct tape. Overnight, you're "the anxious one," "bipolar," or "obsessive", as if your other identities, the cat fanatic, karaoke crooner, disaster cook, simply vanish. The problem isn't the label itself; it's society's reflex to weaponize it.

Internalized stigma prowls like a vengeful housecat. When the world treats you as your diagnosis first and your personhood second, you eventually do the same to yourself. Hope doesn't just dim; it plummets faster than a red-hot penny stock, leaving that flashlight flickering in the abyss.

Diagnostic categories also mutate. Committee tantrums and new research ensure today's disorder may be tomorrow's normal variation. You can cycle through diagnoses you never dreamed of or carry a label that only made sense in 1975. This morphing breeds skepticism toward the DSM's vaunted objectivity. Where is the solid ground when the ground itself shifts?

There's a razor-thin line between ordinary life and clinical pathology. Sad after a breakup? Anxious before public speaking? Exhausted by family at Thanksgiving? Normal. But at what point does normal tip into illness? Over-medicalization is real. We don't need a world where every mood wobble scores a diagnosis, and worse, a prescription. Labels should relieve genuine suffering, not pathologize the full spectrum of being human. Who gets to decide what is normal? After all, what's considered normal for the spider is chaos for the fly, so they say. So, are we spiders or flies? Who can tell anymore?

These labels ripple out into law, insurance, disability benefits, and public policy. Overbroad or misapplied criteria can trap someone in an unwanted identity or erase real pain entirely. Add side effects, iatrogenic harm, and the insidious whisper that "this is just who you are," and suddenly the cure feels worse than the disease. Stakes are so high that person-centred care is no longer optional; communication, consent, and attention to social context are lifelines.

Let's play with the models. The medical model has reigned supreme: people are broken machines needing repair, identify the faulty part, swap it out, reboot. Great for cars; cringe-inducing for the human psyche. It spots symptoms and suggests meds, but context? Invisible. Enter the social model, elbowing medical dominance and whispering, "Wait, maybe your brain's fine; maybe the world is broken." Inaccessible workplaces, crushing stigma, poverty, discrimination, and social exclusion are footnotes in the medical model, but front-page news for the social approach.

Merge them, and treatment blossoms. Biological, psychological, and social factors all count. Medication and therapy plus community support, workplace accommodations, and active stigma dismantling. Brains don't float in vacuums; neither do people. Recovery isn't linear; it's messy, multidimensional, shaped by neurons and neighbourhoods, circuits and society.

Culture complicates this mess even further. A behaviour deemed pathological in one context can be a sacred ritual or normal coping elsewhere. Misinterpret it, and you pathologize someone's lifestyle. Awareness, humility, cultural sensitivity, and mandatory survival skills for anyone diagnosing complexity. Labels are tools, powerful but perilous. Wield them with care, and they illuminate paths to well-being; neglect caution, and they dehumanize, stigmatize, and destroy.

Ultimately, the language of pathology is not sterile jargon but social currency. Our words shape perception, access, and the lives around us, as well as our own. Handle them with humanity, respect, and yes, sardonic humour, and maybe, just maybe, our mental health system might serve real humans. Or we can keep pretending that checkboxes substitute for empathy, and watch the straitjacket tighten a little more.

Reclaiming personal narratives is guerrilla warfare against a system that long defines us by deficits and acronyms. Personal stories assert agency and push back on the pathology lens. Research confirms exposure to recovery tales fosters connection, validation, and hope. Suddenly, you're not a case file but an adaptive, albeit bruised, human. Storytelling becomes resistance, a subversive rebellion against reductive labels.

Peer advocacy delivers the coup de grâce. Programs led by those with lived experience don't just offer sympathy; they hand out survival manuals for navigating the Kafkaesque mazes of modern mental health care. These peers defy the expert hierarchy, proving recovery can be collaborative, relational, and rooted in real life. Reframing the conversation around resilience and social context forces the system to face the uncomfortable truth: mental health is inseparable from society's flaws, poverty, discrimination, and isolation. Surviving these structural failures, not merely managing symptoms, is the true task.

Still, pathologizing normal variation still thrives. ADHD and depression, especially in youth, are overdiagnosed. The expansion of criteria means quirky kids become medical emergencies; stigma gets a bureaucratic boost. History warns us: homosexuality was a DSM disorder until 1973, a societal norm masquerading as science. Today, we see diagnostic inflation and casual labelling in everyday chat, while social factors that shape mental health remain invisible.

This highlights why personal narratives are urgent. Lived experience doesn't just illuminate what it's like to exist in a stigmatized mind; it blasts open the machinery magnifying suffering. Linking distress to economic insecurity, social marginalization, and oppressive workplaces reminds us that mental health floats tethered to real-world forces. Wellness is not an absent diagnosis; it's more like present, supportive environments, equitable resources, and a society that values messy human diversity.

Reclaiming the narrative is a form of rebellion and empowerment. Through storytelling and advocacy, individuals stake their right to self-definition, challenge reductive frameworks, and forge an inclusive, nuanced discourse. Every tale of struggle and resilience jabs at stigma, teaches communities, and stretches society's imagination about living with, rather than under, mental health challenges.

Intersectionality deepens meaning. Marginalized identities add layers of complexity, racism, sexism, and ableism intersect with mental distress. These stories are often silenced. Reclaiming them is not just self-expression; it's survival and a middle finger to a world that prefers neat boxes to human richness.

History reminds us we're not alone in this fight. Early reformers and writers defied medical orthodoxy, proving that narrative is powerful. Nellie Bly's Ten Days in a Mad-House cracked the asylum's moral façade when she feigned insanity to expose abuse. Her voice-based resistance still resonates; lived testimony thunders louder than clinical theory.

Creative arts extend this reclamation. Art, music, literature, performance, lifelines for translating inner landscapes, clinical language erupts to miss. A painting of panic, a song drenched in despair, a play unravelling trauma, they convey dimensions that numb checklists cannot. Creative expression bridges the individual and society without a PhD decoder.

Shared stories ripple across social media, classrooms, and forums, confronting assumptions and blind spots. Communities grow more inclusive, aware, and able to support diverse experiences. When society listens and integrates these narratives, stigma's power cracks. Isolation shrinks; connection blossoms. Mental health shifts from private burden to collective concern.

This is ongoing work, powered by each fresh voice. Reclaiming narrative is a practice of agency, challenging assumptions, and expanding frameworks for understanding well-being. Each story nudges society toward valuing diversity, complexity, and the entwined nature of individual experience and social context. Narrative becomes a catalyst for transformation, a testament to resilience, and proof that our shared humanity resists reductive definitions.

Words matter. Our own and everyone else's. Calling someone "suffering from" depression casts them as passive victims. Saying they're "living with" or "experiencing" a condition returns agency. Linguistic pivots aren't fluff; they reshape legislation, treatment, and daily interactions. The evolution from "mental patient" to "person with a mental health condition" signals society's grudging awakening that how we speak dictates how we think and act.

An integrated approach that melds medical and social models gives us a richer picture of human experience. Biology and psychology count, but societal structures, culture, and environmental accessibility are equally decisive. Yet our society remains lazy about accommodating difference. Schools churn out one-size-fits-all lessons; workplaces reward narrow personality moulds; public spaces overlook sensory diversity. ADHD kids are branded disruptive; autistic adults are labelled unemployable. It's rarely the person at fault; it's the system. But admitting that means toppling neat categories.

Pressure to conform is relentless. From infancy, we're drilled on how to sit, speak, grieve, and even think. Deviate, and you're shoved, or gently steered, into a pathology category. Normalcy bias acts as a psychic straitjacket: deviation is dangerous or immoral. Too expressive, too silent, too energetic, or too reflective, some gatekeeper is tallying your failures.

These pressures are more than abstract. Nearly one in five U.S. adults face mental health conditions, yet only half get treatment. Stigma, self-policing, and systemic barriers make help-seeking an act of bravery. The hidden cost of compliance, masking, social anxiety, and constant self-surveillance is massive yet invisible.

Media fan the stigma flames. Hollywood's schizophrenics swing from peace to homicidal rage in nanoseconds; manic geniuses can't function without meds; reality TV's depressive stirs pity with a vodka glass. News outlets sensationalize suicides sans context; everyday chatter tosses "OCD" and "bipolar" around like spices. Employers, friends, and families internalize these myths and project them onto real people. Meanwhile, those struggling are told they're abnormal, dangerous, and broken, despite data showing people with mental health conditions are far more likely to harm themselves than others. Only 3–5 percent of violent crimes involve mentally ill perpetrators, yet public perception inflates that to living-room-disaster levels.

Cultural bias scripts pathology. Western glorification of stoicism frames expression as weakness; other cultures may invert that. Policies still penalize difference; insurance prefers pills to people; schools mandate one learning blueprint; workplaces punish divergence.

The result: subtle but brutal. Masking is survival, siphoning mental energy from growth and creativity. A 2021 survey found 70 percent of autistic adults plagued by masking-related anxiety; ADHD and other neurodiverse folks show similar patterns. Divergent thinking and high energy, potential strengths, become liabilities in conformity-seeking societies. Society discourages difference, then pathologizes the discomfort it creates. Balanced consistency.

Systemic critiques are unavoidable. Mental health services fixate on crisis over prevention, band-aiding wounds while ignoring the cliffs that caused them. Schools attempt to control behaviour rather than adapt their teaching. Social services, heroic yet underfunded, rarely tackle the economic instability, housing insecurity, and trauma underlying despair and fueling mental crisis. A young adult drowning in precarious employment gets therapy to cope, not a living wage. The message: fix the person to fit society, not vice versa.

Yet a countercurrent surges. Narrative reclamation is resistance. Lived-experience advocates tell stories threaded with social critique and mordant humour, exposing absurdity and cruelty. Peer programs prove that shared experience trumps clinical distance. Blogs, podcasts, and memoirs democratize authority, reframing “case of schizophrenia” as “person navigating psychosis in an unaccommodating world.” This reclamation is political, hammering at the structures that spawned marginalization.

Reclaimed narrative doesn't just humanize, it politicizes. People link distress to exploitative workplaces, housing crises, and historical oppression, framing mental health as a societal responsibility. Imagine tackling unaffordable housing with the same urgency we prescribe antidepressants. Radical, isn't it?

This narrative shift fosters empathy, dismantles stigma, and underscores complexity. Lived-experience stories reveal suffering alongside humour, growth, and love. A diagnosis doesn't erase humanity. Mental illness is constructed through language, culture, and power, yet always contestable. By embracing nuance, scrutinizing norms, and centring lived voices, we inch toward a world that values diversity.

Here's the grand paradox: society's effort to squeeze us into moulds has birthed a shared language of critique, survival, and sardonic laughter. We supposedly abandoned asylums and iron restraints, yet we've swapped physical bars for bureaucratic ones. Padded rooms? Replaced with padded paperwork. Isolation wards? Replaced with waitlists.

Media plays its tragicomic role. Headlines cry "dangers of untreated mental illness," then lobby for harsher commitment laws and more police power. Subtext: mental illness equals public safety threat, until the next PR exhortation to "end the stigma." A self-perpetuating cycle of performative compassion and punitive policy under the banner of "community care."

Pop culture's archetypes still dominate: the "mad genius," the "violent schizophrenic," the "tragic depressive." Viewers glean more from crime dramas than public health campaigns. A 2022 global review found 70 percent of film portrayals link mental illness to violence, even though real-world data says people with mental health conditions are far likelier victims than perpetrators. But "dangerous lunatics" sell popcorn. That can't be emphasized enough.

Compassionate slogans clash with punitive systems and chronic underfunding. We pat ourselves for progress over asylum-era horrors, yet the ghosts persist, cleaner walls, gentler policies, chemical sedatives instead of straightjackets, but containment, nonetheless. When someone declares "we've come far," ask: from where, to what? Progress is relative. Fewer chains; more bureaucracy. Stigma commodified mindfulness apps sold to those denied therapy. The asylum never died; it rebranded.

Modern psychiatry excels at selling the illusion of progress. Lunacy has become "conditions" and "syndromes," civilized, insurable. Suffering gets billing codes: depression is F32.0; schizoaffective disorder is F25.1. Translated into alphanumeric shorthand, pain becomes data for systems, not cries for help.

The irony is brutal: once anguish becomes data, it's easier to ignore. Policymakers spin charts justifying cuts, hospitals tout "better outcomes" to expedite discharges, and suicide rates become bullet points on performance reports. Between the DSM and quarterly audits, humanity vanishes in translation.

Chapter Fourteen
A Problem of Trust

Trust is a polite word for surrender in the mental health care system. It is dressed up as collaboration, painted as partnership, and sold as empowerment, but in practice, it often feels like being asked to hand over your inner life to a rotating cast of strangers holding clipboards and keys. Trust is not gently built here. It is required at intake, documented in consent forms, and implied by the locked door behind you. You are expected to trust not because trust has been earned, but because the alternative is noncompliance, resistance, or worse, a note in your chart that follows you like a shadow.

The system asks for a level of trust that would be considered absurd in almost any other context. You would not tell your most private thoughts to a stranger on a bus, yet you are expected to disclose them fluently in a white room under fluorescent lights. You are asked to recount your worst moments to someone who may be gone in six weeks, reassigned, burnt out, or promoted into administration. You are encouraged to open wounds for the sake of healing, even when experience has taught you that exposure does not always lead to care. Sometimes it leads to restraint. Sometimes it leads to dismissal. Sometimes it leads to a diagnosis that hardens into a permanent identity you did not choose.

Trust in this environment is complicated by power. This is not mutual vulnerability. One party speaks and the other documents. One party cries, and the other codes. One party risks everything by being honest, while the other risks almost nothing by misunderstanding. The imbalance is subtle enough to be denied and absolute enough to be felt in every interaction. You learn quickly that trust is not just emotional. It is procedural. It is knowing which truths are safe to tell and which will cost you privileges, autonomy, or credibility. You begin to edit yourself, not because you are dishonest, but because you are trying to survive.

There is a particular kind of terror that comes with being told to trust the system by the same system that has already failed you. Trust us, they say, while referencing policies you never helped write. Trust us, while explaining that what happened to you was unfortunate but necessary. Trust us, while reminding you that resistance indicates a lack of insight. The language of care becomes indistinguishable from the language of control, and you are left wondering whether trust is a genuine request or simply another clinical expectation disguised as kindness.

For many, the first betrayal is not dramatic. It is administrative. It is the file that follows you without your consent. It is the assessment that reduces complexity into checkboxes. It is the moment you realize that your history has been summarized by someone who met you on your worst day and never saw you on a good one. Trust erodes quietly when you recognize that your narrative has been overwritten by institutional shorthand. You become a risk level, a compliance concern, a treatment-resistant case. The system insists it sees you as a whole person, yet interacts with you as a problem to be managed.

Dark psychology thrives in environments where authority is unquestioned and vulnerability is compulsory. The mental health system does not need villains to be harmful. It only needs routines. Harm becomes normalized through repetition, through handoffs, through the quiet belief that someone else is responsible. You are told to trust the process, even when the process feels designed to break you down into something easier to contain. You are told that mistrust is a symptom, not a response. Suspicion becomes pathology. Self-protection becomes paranoia. The system teaches you that your instincts are unreliable, then wonders why you struggle to trust your own judgment.

There is a particular cruelty in asking people who have already been hurt to place their faith in strangers with institutional authority. Many patients arrive with histories of betrayal, abuse, neglect, or coercion. They are not entering care with a blank slate. Yet the system often treats mistrust as an obstacle rather than evidence. Instead of asking why trust is hard, it asks why trust is absent. Instead of earning confidence through consistency, it prescribes patience. The burden of trust is placed squarely on the person with the least power and the most to lose.

Sarcasm becomes a survival tool. If you cannot laugh at the absurdity of being evaluated for honesty while knowing that honesty is dangerous, you will break. There is something darkly comedic about being told that openness is essential while being punished for saying the wrong thing. You learn to smile during assessments, to soften your language, to present distress in acceptable doses. Too much and you are unstable. Too little and you are minimizing. Trust becomes a performance, and you become an actor in your own treatment.

The haunting part is not just the fear of harm. It is the slow realization that trust is being extracted rather than cultivated. You are expected to comply first and feel safe later. You are told that safety will come with time, once you have proven yourself cooperative. This reverses the basic logic of human connection. In the outside world, trust grows through reliability and care. In the system, trust is the entry fee. If you cannot pay it upfront, you are seen as difficult, guarded, or oppositional.

Working your way through the system requires a kind of emotional endurance that few talk about. Each new provider requires a retelling. Each retelling requires exposure. Each exposure risks misunderstanding. You brace yourself before every appointment, not because you do not want help, but because you know the cost of being misheard. You begin to compartmentalize your story, offering fragments rather than the whole. Trust becomes conditional, negotiated, and fragile. You give just enough to access care, but not enough to lose yourself.

There is also the haunting knowledge that trust, once broken here, is not easily repaired. An error in judgment can follow you for years. A single note can outlive the clinician who wrote it. The system has a long memory for risk and a short memory for growth. You may change, heal, stabilize, and rebuild, yet your file remains frozen in time. Trusting a system that does not forget your worst moments requires a leap of faith that feels more like desperation than courage.

What makes this especially dark is that trust is genuinely necessary for healing. Connection matters. Safety matters. Belief matters. The tragedy is that the system often undermines the very thing it claims to require. It demands trust while operating in ways that discourage it. It preaches transparency while functioning behind closed doors. It speaks of empowerment while retaining unilateral authority. Patients are left navigating a maze where trust is both the key and the trap.

Strangers are not inherently dangerous. Many clinicians care deeply and work within constraints they did not create. But the system does not run on individual goodness. It runs on policies, risk management, liability, and throughput. Trusting a stranger with your inner life is one thing. Trusting an institution with the power to confine, medicate, label, and override is another entirely. The system conflates the two, asking you to extend personal trust into an impersonal structure that was never designed to hold it.

There is a grief that comes with realizing how much bravery it takes just to show up. To sit in a chair and speak honestly when history suggests that honesty can be weaponized. To accept help from people who might disappear without explanation. To keep trying after being dismissed, restrained, ignored, or patronized. This grief is rarely acknowledged. Instead, persistence is framed as resilience, as if endurance were a choice rather than a necessity.

Trust in the mental health care system is not a single decision. It is a series of calculated risks. Each disclosure is weighed. Each appointment is a gamble. Each recommendation is evaluated not just for its benefits, but also for potential fallout. You learn to read between the lines, to watch body language, to note what gets written down. Trust becomes an ongoing negotiation with an invisible audience that may interpret your words long after you leave the room.

The darkest irony is that those who trust easily are often the ones most harmed. Naivety is not protected here. It is exploited by default procedures that assume compliance equals consent. Meanwhile, those who hesitate are scrutinized. The system punishes both extremes, leaving little room for cautious engagement. You are expected to trust perfectly, neither too much nor too little, without being given the rules.

And still, people keep trying. They keep walking back through the doors. They keep telling their stories. They keep hoping that this time will be different. That this provider will listen. This treatment will help. That trust will finally be met with care rather than consequence. This persistence is not a weakness. It is a testament to how deeply humans want to be seen, even in places where seeing is dangerous.

Trust, in this context, is not soft. It is hard-won, bruised, and provisional. It exists alongside fear, not in its absence. To trust the mental health care system is to accept uncertainty as a constant companion. It is important to know that harm is possible and proceed anyway. It is to navigate a landscape where help and danger are often indistinguishable until it is too late.

Perhaps the most honest thing the system could say is, "Do not trust us," but we know that would be terrifying. We know we have power over you. We know we have failed before. We know asking you to believe in us asks more than most people will ever understand. Until that honesty exists, trust will remain what it has always been here. A fragile offering made by those with the least leverage, in the hope that vulnerability will be met with care instead of control.

Chapter Fifteen
Navigating the Modern Asylum

Every morning begins beneath the iron weight of a diagnosis; it's there before your name, etched into a sterile digital dossier that looms like a verdict. Long before anyone offers a greeting, a label whispers in their minds: "the anxious one," "the unpredictable one," "the one who never quite fits." Conversations aren't invitations to connect; they're auditions where you perform the right symptoms, nod at the approved pauses, and hope your humanity doesn't collapse under the glare of assumption. Complexity becomes your undoing; compliance is your only currency. In this realm, simply existing means submitting to a system that measures breath and heartbeat like data points in a prison log.

Clinics, community centers, and hospitals promise sanctuary but deliver surrenders. Every signature on a consent form is a chain link; each checkbox is a reminder that your autonomy is negotiable. Nurses vanish into corridors of insurance codes; appointment requests dissipate in automated phone mazes. Months can slip away while you wait for pre-authorization; pharmacies hold your scripts hostage for weeks. You become part patient, part sleuth, hunting down lost referrals, deciphering billing jargon, and orchestrating a scavenger hunt for the most basic care. Recovery isn't the goal, bureaucracy is.

Therapy, once hailed as a lifeline, often lies tantalizingly out of reach. Waiting lists stretch like cobwebs, and when a slot finally opens, fees soar beyond reach. Public programs give you six or eight sessions as if a dozen half-hours could excavate decades of pain. You're rushed to squeeze insights into prescribed intervals, coached to show "progress" like a quarterly report, as if your mind were a business plan rather than a lifetime of tangled memories. When the clock ticks, the refuge shutter closes, leaving you stranded on a ledge.

Inside psychiatric wards, the revolving door never stops turning. Stabilization means dulling symptoms until they barely flicker, then discharging you back into the chaos that sparked them. "Repeat admissions" is the clinical euphemism; for you, it's just life: partial relief, systemic inertia, return. Social determinants, such as unstable housing and workplace stress, are footnotes nobody cares to read. What counts is pill count, attendance, and the neatness of chart entries. Your personhood dissolves in favour of compliance rates and symptom logs.

Those neat diagnostic labels slip out of hospital doors and cling to you everywhere. Police officers read your file before you open your mouth; social workers talk about you in hushed tones in front of you. Calmly crossing the street can turn you into a potential threat if "risk factors" hover above your head. Express a desire to become a parent and brace for intrusive scrutiny. Apply for a loan and watch your independence questioned. Every routine choice morphs into a negotiation with prejudice.

Medications parade before you as miracles shrouded in side effects: fatigue that feels like a permanent hangover, emotional flatlines that erase joy along with pain, tremors, weight shifts, digestive rebellions, blood pressure spikes, and cognitive fog so thick you can't remember your own birthday. You calculate, then swallow tonight's dose and watch your identity slip further away, or skip it and let anxiety reassert its reign. The fear that every pill is a slow erosion of body and mind gnaws at the last vestiges of relief.

Adherence becomes a full-time obsession. Miss one capsule and you're a "noncompliant" patient, a moral failure rather than a person with questions. Charting doses, monitoring side effects, juggling interactions with other drugs: it's a second job you never applied for. Many doctors, strapped by quotas or paperwork mountains, offer no real guidance. You end up self-regulating in isolation, balancing "effective" against "tolerable" with no one to validate your calculations.

Suggestions of exercise, nutrition, or talk groups vanish in the shuffle, and holistic approaches are considered quaint curiosities. Research budgets flow to high-volume drug trials, not integrative or homeopathic efforts. The old ghost of lobotomies and electroshock still stalks the halls, its legacy of control and containment echoing in today's forced medications and locked wards. You know the history; you carry that distrust like a shield against the next psychiatric decree.

Money, or the lack of it, tightens the vice. Private therapy costs more per hour than many people earn per day. Medication co-pays, counselling bills, license fees: they add up to a daily reminder that care is for those who can afford to chase it. Peer advocacy and community support groups flicker into being, then die for lack of funding, leaving you to cobble together a makeshift network from half-remembered blogs and online forums. Even well-intentioned therapists clock out early to fill out insurance claims; relational trust gives way to transactional necessity.

Law enforcement encounters ring with absurdity. A placid conversation with a known diagnosis can trigger involuntary evaluations or detainment. Regardless of tone or context, the label carries the final say. You learn in bitter moments that compliance is assumed, questions are defiance, and skepticism is punished. Humour, sarcasm, and self-parody emerge as survival tactics, tiny rebellions against an invisible cage.

Every day of life becomes a guerrilla campaign against bias. Cooking dinner, paying rent, balancing a budget: each act is proof you can function, each success an unspoken triumph. Parents endure invasive probes into their fitness; employees must constantly outperform unspoken doubts. Open a bank account and hand over proof of "stability." Every day, self-reliance becomes a covert act of rebellion against a system that reduces you to disorder.

Yet persistence blooms in cracks. You push back against labels, carve space to tell your own story, reclaim narrative authority with fierce tenderness. Survival demands mastering bureaucracy, cultivating resilience, forging alliances, online forums, peer groups, and whispered confidences in clinic hallways. Resistance takes shape in demanding second opinions, refusing to swallow words, posting testimonials, and insisting on informed consent. True courage lies not in charts or diagnoses but in the simple act of breathing on your own terms.

From the moment your diagnosis is entered into the record, it precedes you. "Bipolar," "Schizophrenic," "Borderline" people see the letters before the face, make mental checklists before extending a handshake. Every receptionist, nurse, and resident physician scans for checkboxes; every misplaced form or missing signature becomes a barricade between you and survival. Hospitals, clinics, doctors' offices transform into bureaucratic jungles, records shuffled like deck cards, insurance codes recited like mantras, while you absorb the message: your life is paperwork.

Appointments feel less like therapy and more like interrogations under time constraints. In fifteen minutes, you must distill years of trauma into soundbites that satisfy policy. Therapists glance at clocks, psychiatrists scribble in electronic charts, and you learn to anticipate what they want to hear, masking genuine distress so it fits standard parameters. It's a performance that chips away at authenticity and sometimes sanity.

When therapy does come, it's bittersweet. Waiting lists stretch longer than a year; short-term programs force you to encapsulate grief, anxiety, and psychosis into half-hour capsules, like shipping containers labelled "Progress Urgent." You're urged to produce measurable change before the next billing cycle, fueling guilt if tears still come after session six.

The scarcity of emotional sanctuary magnifies every unhealed wound.

Cost remains the relentless gatekeeper. Publicly funded slots vanish in moments; private practitioners charge enough to make you weigh therapy against rent or groceries. Some turn to peer-run groups or internet chatrooms, but these offer limited solace. The patchwork of assistance feels more like a cruel game, one that only those endowed with time, privilege, and energy can ever truly win.

Running the bureaucracy treadmill is exhausting labour: phone trees that end in dead air, referrals lost in labyrinths, and insurance claims denied for missing codes. Miss a deadline or misfile a document, and your medication refill is frozen; your next session is cancelled. For someone grappling with executive dysfunction or cognitive fog, these administrative pit falls become psychological torture.

Even within healthcare, stigma seeps into every crack. Your physical pain is too often chalked up to "psychiatric symptoms," your bodily complaints minimized or dismissed. Side effects get labelled “psychosomatic,” and you become your own jailer, policing every sign of discomfort. Trust in the care system erodes under the weight of constant disbelief.

Amid this, peer support emerges as a flicker of genuine connection. Real people with real scars share strategies, validate raw feelings, and speak a language unbounded by DSM codes or billing priorities. Those relationships illuminate the chasm between human-centred care and cold, transactional treatment.

Isolation tightens its grip. Long wait times, unpredictable mood swings, and unrelenting prejudice drive wedges between you and friends, family, and coworkers. Loneliness seeps in like night fog: both cause and effect of a world that demands normalcy but offers little accommodation.

Institutional definitions of “recovery” clash violently with lived experience. The system wants linear progress, a neatly rising graph, yet mental health is jagged, cyclical, messy. Relapses get branded as failures, weaving guilt and shame into every setback. Patients internalize the narrative: if I can’t stay “well,” it must be my fault.

Navigating each encounter turns into performance art. You learn to describe symptoms in pitch-perfect clinical language, to dial up affect or dial it down, to recite crisis plans like scripts. This exhausting masquerade depletes energy and erodes authenticity, yet stepping out of character risks neglect or punitive measures.

Scarcity of resources fuels daily frustration. Therapy requests queue for months, medication refills stall, and budgets clamp down on supportive services. This isn't mere incompetence; it's a structural refusal to invest fully in mental health care. Every "no" and every delay are reminders that your survival is rationed.

Is it mind-numbing yet? Even just reading it can be enough to exasperate, but it is life for many... every day, and there is more.

A misdiagnosis can spiral into alienation. You drift from one provider to the next, encountering conflicting theories and treatment regimens that never quite fit. You ask: if these "experts" can't grasp my reality, who can? Doubt blooms into despair, reinforcing the cruel myth that your distress is evidence of personal failure.

Everyday life outside the clinical walls is a minefield. A misplaced word, a shrug, a small lapse in mood control, anything can be recast as evidence of instability. Friends pull away, employers jitter, family members whisper. The presumption of incapacity is a silent drumbeat you carry in every social encounter.

Social withdrawal follows. Invitations go unanswered, calls go unreturned. The emotional energy required to navigate microaggressions and manage impressions becomes too steep a toll. The more you conform to expectations, the more exhausted you are, so you withdraw, perpetuating the loneliness that feeds your symptoms.

Diagnosis-driven treatment creates a hierarchy of legitimacy. Only textbook symptoms get taken seriously; creativity, idiosyncratic coping patterns, and expressive breakdowns risk being pathologized. Being “different” becomes equivalent to being deficient.

Even routine medical care morphs into a battle. You complain of chest pain only to have it reassigned to anxiety. You ache physically but are told it's "All in your head." Each interaction demands you fight to be recognized as a full human being rather than an embodiment of DSM criteria.

Still, resilience flickers. Small acts, such as insisting on a second opinion, gathering peer testimonies, and keeping a record of side effects, become lifelines. You build hidden safety nets of friends, journals, and crisis plans. These acts remain invisible to the system but are vital for survival.

Resistance is both a necessity and a moral imperative. Every question you ask, every boundary you assert, chips away at the illusion that patients exist merely to comply. You organize peer groups, share personal narratives online, and lobby for reform. Each story told is a testament to the human spirit refusing to be erased.

Ultimately, the patient experience lives in dualities: vulnerability and fierce strength, crushing isolation and profound connection, mandatory compliance and subversive resistance. It is ugly, exhausting, heartbreaking, but unequivocally human. Bureaucracies can attempt to define and contain, but they cannot extinguish the spark of individual agency.

The endless surveillance, snap judgments, and procedural detours that haunt daily outpatient life mirror, in miniature, the overt mechanisms of control used behind locked doors. If you can understand how patients navigate bureaucratic mazes outside clinical wards, it is essential to grasp how those same pressures escalate into physical restraint, forced medication, and procedural coercion when walls grow thicker and the stakes higher.

Even amid paperwork and whispered prejudices, anticipation, fear, dread, and resignation linger for what comes next. Miss a session, fail to return a call, or utter a dissenting word, and you risk interventions, gentle or brutal. The line between care and control is razor-thin. Those living with mental health conditions walk that edge every day, one misstep from consequences that ripple far beyond a delayed refill or cancelled appointment.

Many describe the ever-present feeling of being trapped in a system that views them as both vulnerable and dangerous. Responders, officers, and clinicians see the diagnosis before they see the person. Someone with schizophrenia, long subdued, might still be treated as volatile at the slightest tremor of emotion. A quiet sigh or a reflective pause can be misconstrued, erupting into unnecessary escalation. Being defined by a label, not by intention or character, fuels a chronic low-grade panic.

The fear of misinterpretation shapes all choices. Patients hesitate to speak sharply, to question care, even to advocate for alternatives; any spark of resistance might be read as volatility. Conversations, family meals, job interviews become risk assessments: every gesture measured against stereotypes, every smile weighed for "appropriateness." Autonomy feels forever provisional.

Chapter Sixteen
Anatomy of Institutional Trauma

Even after discharge, former patients carry lasting souvenirs of psychiatric wards, bruises, broken spirits, and vivid memories burned into brain tissue. It isn't just individual pathology; it's the cruel choreography of architecture, policy, and understaffed rituals that welds trauma onto the psyche. To call these hospitals "sanctuaries" is a perverse joke. They are gladiatorial arenas of stripped autonomy, sensory bombardment, and the constant thrum of coercion.

Promised as bastions of safety and healing, North American psychiatric units instead deliver a theatre of containment. Beneath peeling paint and flickering fluorescents lie overworked nurses forced into a desperate balancing act, managing dangerous shortcuts over meaningful care. Thin staffing, creaky infrastructure, and regulation-obsessed containment conspire so that seclusion and restraint become as routine as breakfast pills. What was supposed to be a "last-resort" intervention slides easily into a first-response protocol.

Seclusion rooms, often called isolation rooms, are marketed as "interventions of utter desperation"; we're assured they're only used when every other option collapses. In practice, they're the go-to when staffing budgets are tight for therapeutic coaches or when there's no private space to talk someone down. A patient is plunked into a windowless box, stripped of agency, left alone with the unambiguous message: "Your suffering terrifies us." Chemical and mechanical restraints follow the same script: obedience through fear rather than an ounce of collaboration.

For people already scarred by neglect, violence, or prior confinement, being housed in these minimalist rooms can rewrite old nightmares into fresh wounds. Trauma doesn't demand cruelty; it thrives on dread, powerlessness, and the inescapable sense of being cornered. Psychiatric wards feed all three.

The environment amplifies the crisis. Imagine perpetual fluorescent glare grazing the walls, corridors echoing panic, and not a scrap of calm or private refuge. Under this relentless siege, emotional regulation vaporizes. Any uptick in distress triggers the same reflexive response: escalate coercion. And so, the cycle feeds itself, crisis begetting more crisis.

Many units still operate out of relics, ex-tuberculosis sanatoriums, mid-century high-security wings, general-medicine annexes thrust into psychiatric duty. Endless hallways, shoebox rooms, no natural light, zero sensory control. These aren't strategic limitations; they're self-inflicted wounds we'd shrug off as "unfortunate but inevitable." Except they're not inevitable, they're a choice, made every time a budget line bleeds trauma-informed space in favour of four more beds.

The physical plant isn't a passive backdrop; it's a co-author of the patient's recovery, or a cage that writes the patient's suffering in bold. Too often, mental health units cling to the bottom rung of capital budgets because it's cheaper to contain than to comfort, to coerce than to cultivate resilience.

Yet even amid this despair, Canada's recent capital projects flicker with both promises and peril. In Montreal, Philippe-Pinel's gleaming revamp boasts a four-story secure pavilion. Yes, security remains paramount, but PR slides hint at sensory rooms and de-escalation corners behind the locked doors that hold forensic patients. Alberta brandishes four new CASA Mental Health centres, a $110-million nod to trauma-informed youth care, allegedly festooned with voluntary quiet zones. Edmonton's $141-million overhaul teases a "Recovery Community" and "Compassionate Intervention Centre," though the narrative remains tethered to bed counts. In British Columbia, Vernon Jubilee Hospital's forthcoming 44 single-occupancy beds suggest calming enclaves in 2026, if you squint past the safety-first press release. Even Prince Edward Island's new Mental Health and Addictions Campus glows with potential, but only time and design details will confirm if it's healing or just another holding pen.

Collectively, these are the largest national mental health infrastructure investments in history, and public relations discourse gleefully touts beds and square footage while punctiliously avoiding the hard questions: How many trauma-informed spaces are there? How many de-escalation rooms? How many staff are trained in sensory modulation? The answers remain buried deep in bureaucratic secrets.

For advocates, these junctures are life-or-death inflection points. This is the rare moment when design can hardwire healing, or double down on existing wounds. Quiet rooms, multisensory havens, voluntary de-escalation corners can't be fringes reserved for "best practice" press fodder; they must be mandated essentials, welded into capital plans, construction blueprints, and public oversight frameworks.

Loopholes proliferate. Floor plans vanish behind confidentiality. "Trauma-informed design" in glowing press releases often reduces to pastel paint chips or extra windows. The devil of structural inertia lurks behind every unaltered hallway: Hôtel-Dieu de Sherbrooke still confines patients in its 1970s psychiatric wings, with long corridors and isolation rooms left untouched for decades, despite a more modern and frequently upgraded facility in the same network on the other side of the city, minus, of course, any psychiatric services. The CHUS Fleurimont has brand new state of the art surgeries, emergency rooms and NICU, and continued construction, but no psychiatric services. Even hospital expansions from the 60s or 80s remain an offset of old blueprints, designed for crises we no longer face. Patients report a lack of privacy, sterile aesthetics, and zero voluntary calm spaces. These facilities don't just fail to heal; they actively aggravate distress.

And it's not a Canadian aberration. Across North America, repurposed relics hold sway. Classic colonnades and isolating layouts double as surveillance systems. Modern annexes from the 70s and 80s frequently ignore contemporary trauma theory, sensory needs, or emotional regulation.

There are some exceptions. Québec's forthcoming Saint-Jérôme mental health pavilion (2026) wraps its 72 beds around patient-centred recovery, complete with both multisensory and soothing rooms, a blueprint proving that trauma-informed design is no utopian impulse but a deliverable outcome. But such case studies are celebrated as breakthroughs, not baseline necessities. And when they're absent, public discourse barely blinks.

Raw numbers confirm the horror show. In Ontario, nearly 25 percent of psychiatric inpatients endure chemical, mechanical, or solitary interventions. In forensic settings, seclusion rates rocket past 27 percent, with individual episodes dragging over 90 hours. These are not anomalies; they're the systemic norm, where coercion is baked into the bedrock even as "trauma-informed care" decorates policy briefs.

Worse, national reporting is a patchwork of shadows. Ontario reluctantly leads the data parade; most provinces barely lift a fingertip to measure the machinery of coercion. Capital dollars tell a similar grim story: psychiatric upgrades suck up under 15 percent of hospital modernization budgets, while acute and long-term care each swipe 30 to 40 percent or higher. Mental health facilities literally finish last at the capital planning banquet.

The U.S. paints a similar yet contradictory tableau. Fairview Acadia, New York State psychiatric centres, Delaware Psychiatric Center, they all rejoice in comfort rooms and multisensory nooks, plus rigorous staff de-escalation training, slashing restraint and seclusion by over 80 percent. Meanwhile, other sites report restraint rates five to ten times the national average. Ownership quirks, staffing ratios, and entrenched cultures overshadow the policy guardrails.

Canada, free of for-profit motives in theory, remains stuck in a twilight zone of no national infrastructure standards, dizzying provincial patchworks, and oblivious oversight. The result is that harmful environments persist unchallenged, like rust eating through a ship's hull.

Patients internalize this cruel architecture. Overstimulating corridors fuel anxiety, despair, and feeling trapped. Crowding and near-zero therapy time quash any chance for meaning. When escape from pandemonium, constant scrutiny, or proximity to others in crisis is impossible, hospitalization morphs from refuge into a crucible.

The built environment becomes either adversary or ally. When design defaults to containing threats, coercion becomes the lingua franca. In Canada, mental health units have traditionally been the benign neglect, ridden cousin of acute care, underfunded, unstandardized, and unsupervised. Under this regime, geography dictates care: your postal code outweighs your need.

Real reform demands more than compassionate rhetoric. We need mandatory quiet rooms in every psychiatric ward, retrofits of aging facilities, binding national design codes, public dashboards revealing environmental conditions and coercive measure rates. Absent these shifts, psychiatric hospitalization remains a macabre game of musical chairs.

The saga of seclusion, restraint, and coercion unspools as structural neglect masquerading as clinical prudence. Building layouts, staffing ratios, and policies are not neutral; they can transmute care into suffering, healing into mere survival. Until budgets, personnel, and humane spaces align around genuine regulation and recovery, patients will cycle through systems that inflame the very crises they are meant to quell.

Psychiatric hospitals claim to be havens of safety, yet for many patients, they are vaults of fear and disempowerment. Even fleeting episodes of physical or chemical restraint leave psychic scars deeper than the chains themselves. Empirical studies link involuntary confinement to worse post-traumatic stress, higher anxiety, and deeper depression, proof that the "cure" can be as injurious as the malady. For those already stigmatized or marginalized, being bound or isolated becomes a grotesque form of punishment under the guise of protection.

Then there's the revolving door. Rapid admissions, scant therapeutic engagement, and nowhere near enough community support render the discharge only half a rescue. Patients re-enter with fresh distress, and the cycle recommences. Hospitals, front and center, become trauma incubators: the very measures meant to stabilize now produce new suffering, guaranteeing the next readmission.

This cycle isn't the result of clinicians' absent-minded negligence; it's baked into the structural culture of underfunded facilities, antiquated buildings, and policies obsessed with occupancy.

Practice variance between units is glaring. Some have minimized coercion through environmental redesign and de-escalation training; others, starved of staff and space, reflexively clamp down with physical interventions. Coercion isn't fate; it's a choice driven by policy, workforce levels, training, and actual architecture. Absent investment, hospitals will remain institutions of trauma, even with the best meds and therapies on call.

Seclusion, restraint, and coerced intervention are not discrete tactics but symptoms of a system that has failed to align resources, infrastructure, and clinical culture with recovery philosophy. Understanding the full scale, variability, and downstream effects of these practices is vital; any debate ignoring the trauma toll of institutionalization tells only half the story.

In Canada, coercion remains endemic. One in seven admissions involves physical restraint; one in six features seclusion; one in four demands forced sedation. These numbers hide wide variation across provinces, hospitals, and unit types. Some general hospital wards restrain more frequently than exclusive psychiatric hospitals, proof that coercion often flows from facility conditions, not pure clinical judgment.

The first 72 hours of admission are the most dangerous for autonomy. Agitated, psychotic, or manic, patients get shunted into the nearest isolation room or administered sedatives, thanks to thin staffing, no de-escalation areas, and reactive policies. Flawed architecture, resource scarcity, and panic reflexes transform hospitals into crash-test facilities for human stress.

Chemical restraint, the most common coercive measure, is a double-edged sword. While sedation can quash dangerous behaviours, it deepens disorientation, hampers therapy, and shatters trust. Repeat exposure to seclusion, restraint, and forced meds, even in "modern" wards, reactivates trauma pathways, drains agency, and magnifies psychiatric vulnerability.

These bleak truths lay bare Canada's paradox: officially, the nation uses less coercion than its southern neighbour, yet in practice, seclusion and restraint remain rampant, variable, and inseparable from structural constraints: overcrowding, staffing deficits, antiquated spaces, and reactionary policies. True reform demands more than protocol tweaks; it demands reconciling the entire hospital environment to reject coercion as default. That sets the stage for examining human costs: readmission cycles and persistent institutional trauma.

Despite high-minded legal and ethical guardrails, Canadian psychiatric facilities skid between aspiration and execution. Provincial statutes, hospital policies, and forensic guidelines promise seclusion and restraint only as last resorts, complete with incident documentation. Rigorous audits, however, expose gaps: shifting definitions, uneven oversight, and spotty compliance with reporting requirements. The law exists, but lived experiences often sketch a different story, one where coercion persists under the weight of operational pressure.

Readmission stats underscore the tragedy. Thirty-day returns vary from single digits to the low twenties; six- to twelve-month returns climb even higher. The causes are painfully familiar: botched discharge planning, housing instability, co-occurring substance disorders, fractured outpatient networks. Each readmission lands patients back in the same overstimulating, coercive wards, an ever-tightening sorrow spiral.

Even earnest efforts to curb restraint and seclusion falter against limited beds, shifting staff schedules, legacy buildings, and fragmented community care. Short stays, high recidivism, and persistent restrictive measures form a negative feedback loop: scarcity begets containment, which begets trauma, which begets demand for more admissions. Welcome to our Straitjacket Society.

Yet amid this bleak cycle, a radical idea emerges in quiet spaces and sensory havens, not to confine but to support. Soft lighting, soothing colours, natural textures, comfortable seating, even glimpses of nature or gentle soundscapes. These rooms treat agitation not as misbehaviour to punish but as a signal begging for support. Trauma-informed design evidence shows that patients with access to designated calm areas self-regulate faster, endure distress more briefly, and engage more deeply in therapy. In some U.S. hospitals, these spaces correlate with lower seclusion rates, shorter stays, and fewer readmissions.

The contrast is stark. Isolation rooms champion containment, predictability, and staff convenience while trampling autonomy and long-term healing. Quiet rooms invest in agency and comfort, signalling that the ward values recovery over mere management. In an era of shrinking staff, overcrowded halls, and bed pressures, omitting intentional calm zones isn't minor; it's a structural failure that deepens stress, perpetuates trauma, and breaks both patients and staff.

This imbalance has real costs. Patients without calming spaces face higher seclusion and restraint rates and earlier readmissions. Hospitalization becomes an incubator of stress, fatigue, and trauma, feeding the revolving door. Staff morale plunges as they are forced into coercion by spaces that undermine therapeutic work. Simply put, the walls and floors of psychiatric units actively shape patient fates for better or for worse.

The lesson is unambiguous: the absence of quiet rooms is not an architectural oversight but a conscious structural decision that sustains institutional trauma. Wards lacking trauma-informed design doom patients and staff to perpetual distress, sabotaging any claim of therapeutic intent. If psychiatric treatment is to live up to its promise, design must prioritize psychological safety over operational convenience.

The gulf between isolation rooms and therapeutic quiet rooms symbolizes the stakes of hospital reform. Control-first environments broadcast distrust and punishment, ratcheting patient stress to new heights. Recovery-focused spaces cultivate autonomy, self-soothing, and dignity, as demonstrated powerfully by shorter stays, reduced coercion, and lower readmissions. Choosing between these extremes isn't cosmetic; it reflects fundamental institutional values that decide whether hospitalization will perpetuate suffering or spark genuine healing.

Incorporating quiet rooms won't banish emergency seclusion overnight, but it widens the arsenal toward healing over dominance. By repurposing underused offices, small consultation rooms, or idle wings into low-stimulation sanctuaries, hospitals can, at modest cost, improve outcomes, ease burnout, and forge a care-first culture.

Canada and the U.S. showcase how ownership and funding shape psychiatric environments. Canada's public, provincially administered system yields coherent policy but scant capital for trauma-informed design. The U.S.'s mix of non-profit, for-profit, and government facilities spawns wildly divergent incentives: some embrace quiet rooms; others treat them as decorative frills. A patient's chances of finding voluntary calm space or being forced into seclusion depend as much on governance structures as on clinical need.

Both nations lean on coercion when wards are overcrowded, understaffed, or outdated. In Canada, nearly 25 percent of inpatients face seclusion or restraint; in forensic hospitals, rates climb even higher. Despite universal coverage and regulation, legacy infrastructure and scarce therapeutic spaces perpetuate trauma. In the U.S., CMS data show seclusion rates ranging from under 1 hour to ten times that, proof that combining environmental redesign, staff training, and patient participation can slash coercion by up to 82 percent.

The evidence is clear: environmental measures aren't optional extras but essential tools to reduce coercion and foster recovery. Canada's public model provides a foundation of standards but lacks mandated investment in calm rooms and staff training. Meaningful reform demands strategies:

1. Policy & Regulation: Expand provincial and federal guidelines to require dedicated comfort/sensory rooms alongside isolation spaces.
2. Capital Planning: Embed purpose-built calming areas in all new builds and retrofits.
3. Clinical Practice: Integrate trauma-informed care training with strategic use of quiet rooms and patient involvement in treatment plans.
4. Monitoring & Research: Track longitudinal data on calm-space utilization, seclusion/restraint rates, and patient outcomes to drive evidence-based policy.

The U.S. demonstrates that comfort rooms are more than theory; they're concrete interventions reshaping distress into regulation. Canada's sparse examples hamper shared learning, while U.S. case studies link design innovation directly to reduced coercion and improved experiences.

Still, Canada is stirring. B.C.'s Secure Room Standards now endorse trauma-informed de-escalation and preventive calming areas. Québec's Saint-Jérôme pavilion proves sensory and soothing rooms can be integral, not afterthoughts. Risk-management bodies like HIROC champion anti-ligature, humane architecture, and principles underpinning sensory rooms, even where they aren't yet realized.

High-potential projects abound: CAMH's Complex Care and Recovery building, Philippe-Pinel's forensic pavilion, Alberta's CASA centres, Edmonton's Compassionate Intervention Centre, Vernon Jubilee, PEI's new campus. Yet public reports obsess over bed metrics, gloss over details of calm space, and treat design as background wallpaper.

Canada urgently needs standardized metrics to evaluate how well physical spaces support recovery, along with transparent reporting on calm-space access and outcomes.

Canada's nonprofit, publicly funded system avoids profit-driven excesses but suffers from regulatory gaps, patchwork design standards, and opaque reporting, resulting in "quiet stagnation" in which decaying environments trap patients in cycles of containment. The scarcity of documented calm-room initiatives signals a clear call to action: embed voluntary sensory spaces alongside policy reform and staff capacity building to curb coercion and champion recovery.

The alternative is unforgivable. Without mandatory quiet rooms, national design codes, public dashboards, and robust training, psychiatric facilities will remain crucibles of trauma. Patients will continue cycling through belittling admissions, traumatic interventions, and hasty discharges, left to stitch together survival in the long shadow of institutional neglect.

It's time to choose to perpetuate a system built on containment and coercion, or reforge wards into genuine sanctuaries of autonomy, safety, and healing. Because the walls we build around mental health care aren't inert, they speak volumes about our values, and they imprint on every patient who passes through.

Chapter Seventeen
Histories Lessons from Asylums to Today

At its height, moral treatment was a fragile promise, a house of cards precariously built on goodwill and tiny patient rolls. The moment wards burst past their limits, that promise was shattered. Neither the Quaker calm of the York Retreat nor Pinel's visionary routines at Bicêtre could survive a flood of hundreds, then thousands, of souls. Care infrastructure, buildings, staffing models, and daily schedules were never designed to uphold human dignity at scale; they collapsed under their own weight.

Overcrowding and hollowed-out supervision turned healing into control. Compassion's warm language ossified into bureaucratese: "management of the insane," "observation," "containment," "safety first." Walls meant to protect patients became barriers meant to isolate them. Long, lifeless corridors; barren, cell-like rooms; regimented "punishments" disguised as therapies, all inflicted a cruelty subtler than iron chains. Cold, echoing halls eroded autonomy as ruthlessly as any shackles.

Fast-forward to today, and the spectre of those asylums still haunts us. Modern psychiatric hospitals, especially in Canada and the United States, often occupy relics of tuberculosis sanatoriums or military convalescent wards. Their sterile glare, narrow hallways, and lack of genuine spaces for self-soothing echo 19th-century neglect. Quiet rooms and sensory havens exist only as scattered afterthoughts, never as the backbone of care. Capacity pressures, funding hierarchies, and bureaucratic mandates still outweigh the environmental conditions essential for real recovery.

Two centuries after Pinel's shouting, the core conflict endures: containment versus care. Before any clinical intervention, architecture shapes patient experience. Where reformers once walked freely among the ill and tailored each day to their needs, today's staff collide with immovable walls and rigid floor plans. Coercion, through seclusion rooms, physical restraints, or the silent trauma of a harsh environment, remains the default response to agitation, echoing every past asylum failure.

This harsh continuum forces a clear conclusion: our struggle isn't just about training staff, writing better protocols, or developing new drugs. It's about the very bones of care: architecture, environment, community. Until we learn what moral-treatment pioneers understood, namely, that the environment is therapy, the penal logic of these institutions will endure. Patients remain imprisoned not by chains, but by corridors, locked doors, and an institutional will that prizes control over comfort.

Trace today's practice to its 19th-century roots, and the pattern is unmistakable. The promise of humane care has always depended on design, resources, and the guts to act. Progress never arrives by decree; it must be built from the ground up, one corridor, one room, one quiet space at a time.

The relentless march toward medicalization buried the environment and lived experience beneath layers of bureaucracy. As asylums ballooned into vast warehouses, high ceilings and interminable corridors became instruments of control. Barred windows, segregated rooms, regimented schedules: all conspired to remake humans into manageable bodies. Surveillance replaced empathy; observation rooms supplanted shared lounges; staff interactions turned procedural rather than relational. The moral treatment ethos of dignity and engagement drowned in a sea of objectivity and paperwork.

Then the pharmacological revolution swept in. Psychotropic drugs promised rapid symptom management and gave administrators the perfect excuse to ignore social and environmental therapies. Healing gardens, art rooms, multisensory sanctuaries, all central to moral treatment, were sidelined in favour of pills and check boxes. Treatment became charts and measurable outcomes, with virtually no regard for the cold of the walls, the glare of the lights, or the echoing emptiness of the halls.

Today's psychiatric wards, often housed in those same old edifices, still bear this legacy. Locked doors, rigid routines, and barren lounges keep stress and agitation simmering, driving more seclusion and restraint. Even new facilities, gleaming with modern finishes, too often prioritize bed counts over therapeutic spaces, tucking comfort rooms into blueprints as optional afterthoughts rather than essential elements.

This arc, from garden walks to psychotropic dominance, from moral engagement to managerial oversight, reveals a grim truth: the more we treat mental illness as a technical problem to be managed, the more our environments become agents of coercion. Despite medical advances and trauma-informed ideals, structural and environmental forces still shape patient lives, echoing centuries-old failures.

Yet moral-treatment lessons never wholly vanished; they were buried under decades of institutional inertia. Today, navigating mental health services often feels like running a gauntlet of iron bars: insurance approvals, eligibility screenings, months-long waitlists, fragmented care networks. Every bureaucratic hurdle acts as a subtle restraint before any therapy even begins. Legal frameworks compound this, too, commitment statutes, guardianship laws, criminal justice intersections, all invisible walls that impinge on autonomy. One minor misstep can trigger interventions far harsher than society would tolerate for anyone else.

The outcome is predictable: countless people with mental health conditions are funnelled into jails rather than treatment centers, extending the legacy of containment under a modern guise. Stigma and social fear erect unseen fences, such as fear of judgment, employment discrimination, and housing insecurity, all of which push individuals to hide their struggles and avoid seeking help. Economic realities, therapy costs, medication bills, unstable incomes- erode freedom and agency, ensuring that structural oppression, though subtler than chains, remains a defining feature of contemporary care.

Even deinstitutionalization, long hailed as liberation, proved a double-edged sword. Without robust community support, many were cast into homelessness or criminalization. New forms of confinement simply replaced the old, and "humane" facilities still rely on surveillance, locked wards, and inflexible schedules, impeccably dressed in a palatable veneer.

Language deepens this oppression. Diagnostic labels, deficit-focused jargon, and sensationalist media narratives reduce complex human lives to symptoms on a checklist. Reformers, faith-based groups, survivor movements, and organizations such as NAMI and MHA have fought fiercely for patient rights. Their victories, though uneven, shine as beacons, each generation inheriting both progress and unfinished battles for dignity, autonomy, and humane treatment.

Seen through this historical lens, today's mental health system stands as the direct heir to the asylums of old. Locked doors, labyrinthine bureaucracies, sterile hallways, they all whisper a continuity of control. Unless we consciously break these patterns, the failures of the past will shape patient lives for centuries more.

The historical arc, from chains to moral treatment, through medicalization, pharmacology, and modern advocacy, reveals a relentless cycle: reform, regression, renewed control, and another burst of advocacy. The past never truly disappears; it lingers in bureaucratic forms, security protocols, societal prejudices, and even in the medications intended to heal.

This is our challenge: to rescue the core wisdom of moral treatment, its insistence on dignity, environment, and community, from oblivion, even as scientific progress advances. We must ensure that today's policies, practices, and architecture do not merely echo past containment but instead forge spaces of safety, empowerment, and genuine recovery.

History offers both a warning and a blueprint. The brief triumphs of moral treatment, the victories of survivor movements, and the spread of trauma-informed care show that systems can bend toward humanity when courage, resources, and design align. Now, more than ever, our task is not just to critique but to create: to imagine and build emancipatory care environments where patient autonomy, trauma-informed support, and real recovery stand at the center. Only then can we break the cycles of coercion, regression, and marginalization that have defined mental health care for centuries and finally fulfill the promise that moral-treatment pioneers set before us.

Chapter Eighteen
Toward Emancipatory Approaches

The failures of our mental health "care" system have never been mere logistical hiccups; these are structural rot, baked into every corridor, policy, and whispered justification. We plaster over gaping wounds with slogans about compassion and reform, but the bone beneath remains fractured. How can we speak of community integration when decent housing is as rare as mercy, when a paycheck is a mirage for most with a diagnosis, and therapy appointments are rationed like contraband?

We stuff bodies into overcrowded wards or punt them to crisis lines like hot potatoes, leaving them to navigate a maze of underfunded programs with no compass. Autonomy? That's a cruel joke pulled on distressed people who must plead for services, then endure zero-continuity care as staff turnovers churn their lives like grindstones. The infrastructure of care, the buildings, the staffing ratios, the social scaffolding, is every bit as critical as that glossy DSM-5. Without it, "recovery" remains a hollow aspiration, autonomy a cruel illusion.

Any talk of emancipation demands we redefine "support." It is far too modest to claim success by reducing the use of seclusion rooms or propping open opaque doors. True care must revolve around agency, dignity, and genuine choice. We must demolish the sensory deprivation cells in our minds and on our hospital floors, replacing them with trauma-informed design, quiet chambers lit by soft daylight, peer-run lounges offering coffee and solidarity instead of chemical restraints. Flexible therapies must be as basic as breathing; consistent community resources should not feel like a luxury but a necessity. When someone can regulate their own rage in a padded nook, have a say in their treatment plan, text a peer-support specialist at 2 AM, or simply sit in a courtyard among other flawed human beings, coercion loses its teeth. Evidence doesn't hide spaces that weave clinical care with social warmth slash distress admissions, seclusion events, and that grim carousel of readmissions.

Policy and advocacy must enshrine these principles in blood-red ink. Provincial, state and federal mandates should demand patient-regulated "chill" zones in every psychiatric wing. They should bankroll neighbourhood programs that do more than patch crises; they must cultivate prevention. Peer-led models? Nonnegotiable. Transparency? Mandatory: publish building blueprints, staffing ratios, therapy access rates, and patient-reported outcomes like you'd sell stock to investors. No more laundering failure with cosmetic "reform." We need to build literal and metaphorical spaces where mental health care is a scaffold that empowers, not a cage that controls.

Let's be brutally clear: care is never neutral. Every tile, every policy, every guarded entry either shackles or frees. Centring human dignity, respecting that every person is more than a diagnostic code, charts a course away from coercion and containment. History's lessons are etched in blood and despair: without intentional design, sufficient funding, and unwavering commitment to autonomy, we perpetuate the same nightmares. But with guts, ingenuity, and relentless advocacy, emancipatory care can flip that grim legacy on its head, forging mental health systems that actually serve the people they claim to help.

Consider Assertive Community Treatment teams, theoretically brilliant, multidisciplinary beacons, promised to reduce hospitalizations by twenty to forty percent while improving social outcomes. On paper, they read like utopia. In practice, they collapse under the weight of systemic neglect. One caseworker juggling twenty high-risk clients? There's no midnight miracle phone line, no extra hands to chase a crisis. Engagement becomes spotty, and burnout is inevitable. That's heroic underperformance, hard-wired into the structure of supposed progress. Even the most advanced interventions are only as potent as the scaffolding that supports them.

Housing initiatives fare no better. Supported housing sounds liberating until zoning boards barge in with their NIMBY torches, underfunding gnaws away at programs, and eviction notices arrive like execution warrants. For every success story of stable apartments and meaningful jobs, there's another tale of isolation, bounced checks, and neighbours calling the police instead of the landlord. Roughly a quarter of people experiencing chronic homelessness report serious mental health conditions; in some cities, that figure soars to forty percent. Integration of clinical and social supports isn't optional; it's urgent.

What do we learn here? Lofty theory means nothing if resources and infrastructure trail behind like ghosts. Emancipatory care isn't a catchy slogan for grant applications; it demands sustained structural investment so autonomy, dignity, and recovery can actually take root. Housing, clinical oversight, social supports, and crisis response must march in lockstep rather than stumble in isolated silos. Only then can community-based programs transcend coercion to deliver genuine empowerment, forging escape routes from the endless loop of crisis and containment.

Look closer at employment programs like Individual Placement and Support. Competitive work is heralded as the path to dignity, yet the labour market treats mental health disclosure as an act of self-immolation. Flexible schedules, occasional absences, a touch of compassion? Absent. A 2021 National Alliance on Mental Illness survey found that sixty percent of employees with serious mental illness hide their diagnoses to dodge discrimination. The system cherishes autonomy, while the workplace punishes difference.

Recovery-oriented care proclaims a fulfilling life despite mental health challenges, with peer specialists guiding the way. Their lived experience is gold, validating, guiding, modelling resilience, yet funding shortages, swelling caseloads, burnout, and stubborn stigma clip their wings. Trauma-informed care, in theory, is straightforward: avoid retraumatization, honour safety, choice, collaboration, and empowerment. In reality, it crashes into rigid protocols, understaffed teams, and waitlists that stretch for months, turning ideals into dusty artifacts.

Words themselves are interventions. Ditch "non-compliant" and ask instead: why did they miss the appointment? Anxiety, no bus fare, a prior nightmare at that clinic? Swap "manipulative" for curiosity: are they seeking human connection or expressing despair? Language frames reality: misapply it, and you pathologize and alienate. Research in Psychiatric Services shows that clinicians who use collaborative, nonjudgmental language achieve higher engagement and adherence, proof that communication can sustain control or ignite empowerment.

Then we have the physical environment, which either bolsters or betrays these efforts. Chaotic, fluorescent-lit waiting rooms ramp up panic; calm, private spaces with sensory tools, soft lighting, noise dampeners, and fidget gadgets whisper safety. Even seating matters: a chair facing the exit sings of agency; one with your back to the door screams vulnerability. Thoughtful trauma-sensitive design cuts agitation, self-harm incidents, and perceived coercion. "Just swivelling a chair so someone could see the exit was the difference between a breakdown and breathing room." These tiny environmental shifts, paired with compassionate language and practice, reveal emancipatory care as far more than heroic programs; it's the delicate alignment of built space, social context, and communication with human dignity.

Remember, healing isn't linear, its been said before throughout these chapters. Relapse isn't failure; it's a predictable reaction to triggers, stressors, and life's bloody roller coaster. Trauma-informed care preaches patience, persistence, and self-care for practitioners' emotional labour, which is real and often ignored. But note how bureaucratic mazes force individuals to rehash trauma endlessly: each retelling is a fresh wound. Streamlined intake, consent-driven information sharing, trauma-sensitive complaint routes, these aren't niceties. They're essential girders for safety and dignity.

Co-production stands as a hallmark of emancipatory care. People with lived experience must hold real seats at the tables that shape services: designing, implementing, and evaluating. Their insights aren't optional decorations; they're lifelines to reduce harm, ensure relevance, and foster ownership. True emancipation is active participation, not passive receipt. Safety, trustworthiness, choice, collaboration, and empowerment aren't corporate buzzwords. They're actionable tenets that transform engagement, reinforce therapeutic alliances, and improve outcomes. In a system designed for control, systematically embedding these principles challenges entrenched hierarchies, thrusting agency back into the hands that have long been denied it.

Advocacy for systemic change is the next charging line. Trauma-informed care alone is a half-measure without policy and legislative backup. Mental health parity is still a mirage: insurance and public funds still relegate mental health to the back row behind "real" medicine. Discrimination crawls through employment, housing, education, courts. Behaviours born of illness, public intoxication, destitution, and crisis episodes are fast-tracked into the criminal system. Emancipatory approaches demand robust alternatives: diversion programs, mental health courts, and rights-based frameworks that preserve autonomy while connecting people to meaningful care.

Several U.S. cities have proven that mental health courts can slash repeat arrests for people with serious psychiatric diagnoses while boosting service engagement, a blueprint reminding us that justice and humanity need not be at odds.

Equally critical are community-based services and supportive housing. Stable housing is not a luxury; it is the bedrock of recovery. Wrap-around models, knitting together clinical care and social supports, reduce homelessness, cultivate safety, and give individuals a platform to rebuild. Yet the finest programs founder without guidance from those with lived experience. Token consultations won't cut it. Expertise drawn from survival in the trenches must helm advisory boards, task forces, research, and program design. Otherwise, we risk recycling well-meaning policies that stealthily perpetuate exclusion or worse, coercion.

When woven together, trauma-informed care, emancipatory policy, community-based supports, and centring lived experience form the architecture of a genuinely liberatory mental health system. The road ahead is neither brief nor bloodless, but it is navigable if we stare down embedded power dynamics, shatter systemic stigma, and commit to tangible, accountable change. Only by uniting infrastructure, practice, and advocacy can we transition to a paradigm that truly prizes dignity, agency, and meaningful recovery.

We cannot ignore the social determinants of mental health, poverty, racism, discrimination, educational inequity, and environmental hazards. Policy advocacy must extend beyond clinic walls into the broader battleground of social justice. Anti-racist laws, economic fairness, equitable education, and environmental protections, these are mental health policies. True emancipation is inseparable from social justice. A 2020 survey found Black and Indigenous people were twice as likely as white peers to report unmet mental health needs due to structural barriers, a grim reminder that systemic inequity is itself a mental health crisis.

The tools of advocacy are many: shock-value public campaigns, unflinching media engagement, grassroots mobilization, lobbying, letter-writing, legal challenges, and impact litigation. Progress is slow, maddeningly so. Coalitions matter. Sustained inclusion of those most affected is nonnegotiable. Our aim: a society that recognizes mental well-being as a human right, undergirded by policies and practices that champion equity, dignity, and opportunity.

At the heart of emancipation lies individual empowerment. Mental health systems must pivot from paternalism to partnership, acknowledging people as experts in their own lives. Shared decision-making, clear consent, accessible information, transparent options, and respect for refusal aren't politely optional. They're foundational. Recovery belongs to the individual, not a clinician's tick-box: rebuilding relationships, pursuing creative passions, forging purpose, navigating life on one's own terms.

Emancipation is neither a theory nor a luxury; it's a mandate for systemic upheaval, social justice, and unwavering devotion to autonomy. Our next challenge: topple lingering barriers of stigma, dismantle deficit-focused narratives, and uproot the insidious ways language and perception constrict our understanding of mental health.

Restrictive practices, such as handcuffs, seclusion, and forced medication, must be exceptional, subject to merciless scrutiny, and deployed only when every other humane option has failed. Safety is nonnegotiable; control must never substitute for connection. Architectural details can cage or free: shaping recovery as surely as any pill.

Continuous evaluation, feedback loops, and the integration of lived experience are vital to ensure services stay empowering rather than stagnate. Peer support offers irreplaceable validation; lived insight is a cornerstone for hope, self-efficacy, and agency. Life skills training, vocational programs, education, creative engagement, they don't pad resumes. They breathe purpose, bridging the chasm between care and true independence.

Emancipatory mental health care is more than a catalogue of interventions; it is a philosophy rooted in human rights, respect, and dignity. Individuals are active agents, not passive recipients. Services must honour their voices, value their choices, and safeguard self-determination. Systems should flex, adapt, and center empowerment as their guiding north star. True emancipation knits together personal healing with systemic reform, toppling paternalistic edifices while cultivating resilience and flourishing. It demands the co-creation of environments, clinical, social, and societal, where mental well-being and self-governance are inseparable, and where people are empowered to lead meaningful, purposeful lives.

Even the noblest emancipatory intentions can founder on the reefs of legal loopholes, economic pressures, and invisible stigma straitjackets. You might exit a supportive housing program with a sense of hope, only to collide with unyielding landlords, bureaucratic roadblocks, and an employment market that demands silence about your history. Liberation in mental health thus transcends services; it requires tearing down the structural, cultural, and social chains that quietly decree who may thrive and who must suffer.

Chapter Nineteen
The Doctors We Leave Behind

If the invisible straitjackets are the walls of the modern asylum, then doctors are the gloved hands of the system pressing against those walls, tightening them ever so politely, as though no one is meant to notice the slow crush. We are sold the notion that doctors hold the key to healing, that they stand at the cusp of science and compassion, but that belief is a carefully manufactured illusion, a marketing slogan that distracts from the truth: an overwhelming majority of physicians have surrendered to the machinery. Only a rare few still cling to the idea that medicine is a vocation rather than an assembly line. The rest, well, let's be frank: give up. They fold. They stop listening. They become part of the conveyor belt that dumps out one traumatized patient after another, each more broken, more voiceless, than the last.

When a patient finally shuffles into the doctor's office, they don't bring just symptoms on a clipboard. They haul in silent luggage stuffed with months or years of waiting lists; with phone trees that hang up on distress; with crisis lines that place them on indefinite hold until they can no longer recall why they needed help in the first place. They lug trauma, distrust, the fear of judgment, and the bitter memory of being ignored or pathologized. Every person arrives like an unshaped lump of clay, already cracked by a system built not to heal but to corral, to label, to render compliant. They are expected to unload it all clearly and concisely in a span of fifteen minutes, fifteen wildly inadequate minutes (on average). A doctor is supposed to establish trust, listen, comprehend, diagnose, and document it all for the paperwork gods who value ticked boxes over breaths saved. Fifteen minutes to face despair, to stare down trauma, to confront raw terror and still emerge unscathed, or at least with something that looks like care. After fifteen minutes, the conversation shifts to medications, follow-up needs, additional testing or treatments and appointment scheduling before the next patient in line is shuffled in.

The first cruelty is numbers. In many regions of Canada, there is one psychiatrist for every 20,000 people; the United States braces for a predicted shortage of more than 14,000 psychiatrists in the coming years. In rural counties, they may find none. Where doctors do exist, they are a commodity scraped thin across an abyss of need. They handle hundreds of cases, juggling complex comorbidities, medication adjustments, therapy referrals, emergencies, and mountains of insurance paperwork. Twelve-hour days bleed into fourteen-hour nights. Burnout is a foregone conclusion. Yet the suffering of patients does not take pity on physician schedules. Every nuance missed, every question unasked, every symptom overlooked festers into fresh wounds. These figures, one per 20,000, projected 14,000 missing, are not mere statistics. They stand as a public confession: we will tolerate quiet, systematic human suffering, then feign shock when people finally break.

The second cruelty is procedural absurdity. Efficiency equals care is the mantra, an assertion as logical as claiming that straitjackets equal freedom. A doctor can shuffle thirty patients through a single day, check every institutional box, input every billing code, and then feel a hollow pride in productivity, while their patients leave trembling, misunderstood, only half-diagnosed, or retraumatized anew. “Press one for medication refills, press two for therapy referrals, press three if you're still suicidal", this is the Kafkaesque tune humming beneath every appointment. Time is not a stream but a cage, and the more a patient thrashes inside, the more they are tacked with damning labels: resistant, noncompliant, difficult. Each term is a bolt tightening around autonomy. This absurdity isn't an accident; it is engineered, structural, a form of bureaucratic cruelty masquerading as clinical best practice.

Then there is transference, the murky, uncanny dance of two wounded minds that no checklist can account for. A patient, braced by history to expect disbelief, steps into the office like a soldier poised for gunfire. Fear registers as anger; grief flares into defiance; anxiety snaps into hostility. The doctor reads pathology in these survival responses symptoms to be slotted, controlled, and medicated. The patient reads detachment in the doctor's clipped tone and diverted gaze, proof of indifference, suspicion, threat. A downward spiral ensues; a private psychological torture chamber built from past traumas and institutional design. Two people, both constrained, fail to meet because the system optimizes for throughput, metrics, and liability rather than for shared humanity. When that failure lands, who carries the weight? Always the patient, the one who dared to hope. Their nervous system tightens, their trust bleeds away, their last spark of hope dims.

A handful of doctors attempt real empathy. They tiptoe through a minefield of policy, liability, and paperwork with genuine care, pushing back against overwhelming currents. But they are the rare exceptions. Most doctors either collapse into the machinery, learning to speak the language of checkboxes and diagnostic codes, or they retreat into apathy. Some become brusque, dismissive, even outright cruel. I've encountered physicians who barked at their patients, blamed them for their own illnesses, and scoffed at fear, anxiety, and despair. These moments are not glitches in the matrix. They are natural emergences from a system that punishes patience, upholds speed over understanding, and smothers human suffering under layers of policy language. Each shouted word, each dismissive wave, every clinical footnote marking a patient “noncompliant” inscribes fresh trauma into that person’s psyche, carried forward into the next room, the next appointment, the next crisis. With every interaction, the unseen straps of the straitjacket pull tighter across the collar, the chest, and the wrists.

Yet, astonishingly, patients still return. They persist, shattered but stubbornly alive, despite appointments fragmented across multiple offices, referrals that vanish into bureaucratic black holes, and doctors who simply cannot or will not meet them fully. Each encounter becomes a harsh curriculum: to be worthy of attention, one must perform, prove, present suffering in a sanitized form, calibrate language to suit policy, and contain the chaos within strict boundaries. When the system predictably fails, when emergency services are summoned, involuntary hospitalizations occur, when the sick leave runs out, the patient emerges diminished. Hope is rationed, autonomy questioned, and pain reinterpreted as self-inflicted pathology. Every procedural step, every checkbox tick, every line in the chart reinforces containment and erodes genuine care.

Documentation, too, becomes its own cruelty. A patient may recount panic attacks, suicidal ideation, chronic despair, traumatic history, a soul laid bare, only to see it reduced to risk assessment scores, diagnostic codes, and a standardized medication plan. Complexity is erased. Nuance is discarded. Noncompliance is logged as a character flaw rather than an expression of mistrust, fear, or past neglect. The system claims this is neutral, clinical language, but its effect is punitive. Each bureaucratic demand for proof or justification adds another bar to the invisible straitjacket. Kafka himself might have applauded the architecture of referrals, appointments, and paperwork: one form demands evidence of crisis to unlock care, another penalizes the very articulation of distress. Each office, each policy, every so-called best practice quietly ensures that patients must navigate a labyrinth simply to be heard. And even after they manage that feat, relief is fleeting. The next referral, the next appointment, the next insurance hurdle looms ready to erase the fragile trust built in the last encounter.

The system is unrelenting. It is absurd. It is cruel, and, crucially, entirely legal. Every patient story reads like an indictment: “It felt like screaming into the void,” “I might as well have been talking to a chatbot,” “She never even looked me in the eye.” These are not poetic flourishes. They are precise evidence, human data, raw and uncompromising. Each encounter twisted, each concern dismissed, every file left unread: they are bolts drawing tight around human potential. Trauma piles up. Hope caves in. Nervous systems contract. Autonomy retreats into hiding. The invisible straitjacket is woven not from leather straps or iron chains, but from language, policy, time scarcity, systemic mistrust, and fear.

The real tragedy? None of this is necessary. None of it is inevitable. In theory, doctors could choose another path: listen without the digital clock ticking behind their eyes, trust without the threat of liability flickering in their periphery and respond with curiosity rather than pre-emptive judgment. But the system conspires against them and their patients at every step. Bureaucracy prizes efficiency, not empathy. Liability demands caution, not courage.

Metrics enforce documentation, not human connection. The patient suffers first, and then the physician suffers, trapped in a loop that measures the wrong outcomes. Even the most compassionate doctor can only swim against these currents for so long.

The invisible straitjacket is not a mere metaphor. It is operational, enforceable, woven into every forty-five-minute appointment grid, every insurance code, every referral loop, every line in a patient's chart. Until we reimagine the system; until time, trust, empathy, and understanding eclipse efficiency, order, and compliance; until we dismantle mechanisms that reduce living, breathing people into processed data, until then, patients will keep arriving diminished, and leaving smaller than they began. Trust will remain a scarce commodity. Recovery will stay perilously fragile. Human potential will continue to be contained, policed, and penalized, dressed up in the language of necessity and justified as care.

The few doctors who resist this tide of indifference are islands in a flooded bureaucratic world. They sink slowly under the weight of policy and paperwork, or they become exhausted beacons flickering out. Most are lost long before they can make a dent. The rest well, they fall back on sarcasm and dark wit, on efficient cruelty dressed as clinical detachment. They have learned language as armour, discipline as detachment. Their mistake, ironically, is believing they must survive by hardening their hearts. And so, they do.

Until we confront this reality head-on, until we tear down the invisible walls, pry open those gloved hands, and demand that human connection reclaim its place at the core of care, we remain complicit in cruelty. We have not reformed the system; we have merely repackaged, polished, and renamed it. And every patient who dares to hope carries the burden of that betrayal into the next doctor's office, into the next crisis, into the next day, always hoping, against every reason, that this time will finally be different.

Chapter Twenty
Society Without Invisible Straitjackets

Every morning, we wake up tangled in unseen chains. The faint sting of a coworker's backhanded compliment. The dismissive "just follow the protocol" from doctors who see your name as an account number. The endless maze of benefit forms, each page a trapdoor meant to break your will. We plaster slogans like "evidence-based policy" and "risk management" across conference rooms, but in reality, those words translate to handcuffs. "Patient-centred care"? Spare me. True authority still sits with insurance adjusters, policy wonks, and committee members who've never felt their minds ignite with terror at 2 a.m. or navigated a healthcare system designed to ignore them.

Let's call these straitjackets what they are. Name them. Mock them. Rant in furious tweets until your thumbs blister. Awareness alone won't set you free, but it's the spark that lights the fuse. When people with lived experience take real power by authoring policies, chairing boards, and supervising budgets, change explodes. Padded sensory rooms morph into genuine sanctuaries. Employers finally accept that "9-to-5" can mean 11-to-7. Community housing appears without mandatory "check-ins," curfews, or drug tests. No strings. No shame. Just a roof and respect.

Policy can't pretend these realities are optional. Mental-health parity can't be a clever ad campaign; it must be law, audited by watchdogs, enforced with teeth that bite. Access can't hinge on your neighbourhood or how fat your wallet is. Housing, work, and education resources must be designed around actual human suffering, not lobbed on as disappointing scraps. We don't need another half-hearted committee or glossy brochure. We need policies that charge in with shovels, upturn every cliché, and declare war on neglect.

Criminalizing crises is disgustingly cruel. Handcuffing someone during a panic attack or psychotic break is as humane as throwing a drowning swimmer back into the sea to "toughen up." Instead, we demand diversion courts staffed with mental-health pros, mobile crisis teams riding silently in unmarked vans, first responders trained to soothe instead of subdue. Control is not care. Chains are not compassion. It's time to defund the police as the primary crisis squad and invest in humans who heal, not those who punish.

Culture is not some nebulous backdrop; it's the echo chamber that reinforces every doubt and dropkick of dignity. The whisper that "you're broken" must be drowned out by a roar: "You are complex. You are capable." Teach kids that emotions are neither weaknesses nor weapons to be used against them. Curiosity and sorrow carry gifts if we know how to open them. Design workplaces that treat variation as normal, not an inconvenience. Build neighbourhoods that catch us when we fall instead of posting "No Loitering" signs around despair.

Our current system? Absurdist theatre with real casualties. Medication compliance receives a standing ovation. Waiting lists are eternal. "Choice" in care means picking your flavour of bureaucratic purgatory. Yet every peer-led workshop, every co-designed policy, every raw community art project that refuses to sterilize suffering chips away at the absurdity. These aren't fringe pursuits; they're the front line. They're proof that when lived experience drives design, people don't just survive, they flourish.

Redefine "effective care." If your grand solution still looks like prescription pads and rushed fifteen-minute check-ins, you're managing side effects, not promoting recovery. Sure, therapy and medication can save lives, but they're not magic bullets. Chronic stress, poverty, isolation, unstable housing: these are the wildfires feeding mental-health crises. Treating the brain while letting life burn around it is like mopping up floodwater without turning off the busted pipe.

The data doesn't lie. Secure housing cuts hospital admissions. Meaningful employment slashes depression and anxiety. Creative expression, such as painting, writing, and drumming, measurably lowers stress hormones. These aren't optional extras. They're vital infrastructure. Anything less is minimalism masquerading as care. Checklist-driven programs that ignore community support are gilded cages. Therapy without practical assistance is a lecture on sinking. Medication without autonomy becomes a pharmaceutical straitjacket.

When done right, the outcomes roar. Canada's Housing First placed people in permanent homes with zero preconditions and paired them with peer support. Hospital stays plummeted, and quality of life skyrocketed. Online peer platforms like 7 Cups sprouted in rural areas and stigma-shy communities, giving hope on demand. People flock to help when it's humane, offered by those who've been there, not robotic intake clerks reading scripts.

Language and policy built these straitjackets; they can unmake them. Words that pathologize tighten our restraints; strength-based language loosens them. Structural bias hides in "policy" that steers a crisis toward jail instead of a bed, suspends students for expressing distress, or penalizes workers who ask for simple accommodations. Equity isn't polite; it's a nonnegotiable necessity.

Public art, guerrilla theatre, participatory workshops, these aren't decorative. They're direct action, confronting stigma on streets, in boardrooms, and in living rooms where shame festers. When people with ongoing mental-health challenges run businesses, raise families, and create art, they shatter the deficit-driven myths that clip wings. Strengths-based policies let them soar.

The fiscal stakes are brutal. Untreated mental illness costs over a trillion dollars from the global economy every year in productivity losses. Every dollar we invest in mental health returns four dollars in economic gain. Supported employment, vocational rehab, and integrated care are investments, not expenses. Underfunding is a policy choice that tightens our chains. If we bemoan cost yet starve mental-health infrastructure clinics, crisis teams, and peer networks, we're complicit in the cruelty.

Education and empathy drive liberation. Mental-health literacy must be part of every classroom, boardroom, hospital, and briefing room. Teachers need tools to distinguish between defiance and distress. Managers must spot burnout before it erupts. Police and clinicians should learn de-escalation before reaching for handcuffs. Media must swap sensational headlines for honest stories. When mental health is recognized as a universal human condition, stigma rots, and the invisible straitjackets break open.

The World Health Organization's shift from a narrow "disorder" model to a broad "well-being, functioning, and social context" paradigm shows the path. Outcomes improve, and people actually seek help. Strip shame from treatment and hiding becomes pointless. Words matter. Your snarky office joke, that "harmless" meme, your thoughtless tweet, they either cinch the straps tighter or crack the door of possibility wide open. Choose carefully, unless you're nostalgic for metaphorical thumb screws.

Beneath the chatter lies systemic bias. Incarceration has become a de facto mental-health institution. Schools suspend kids instead of supporting them. Employers show the exit door to employees asking for accommodations. This structural cruelty isn't accidental; it's baked into the design. Equity is not optional; it's the floor, not the ceiling.

Canada's National Standard for Psychological Health and Safety in the Workplace offers a blueprint: concrete guidelines that eradicate discrimination, cut absenteeism, and boost retention, proving dignity and profit are not enemies. It's not rocket science; it's common sense. Language reform and structural overhaul converge on one truth: these straitjackets aren't accidents or byproducts of complexity. They're choices made in boardrooms, agencies, and comment threads. Our mission: stop manufacturing them altogether.

Imagine a world that doesn't just manage distress but refuses to shackle it socially, linguistically, or structurally. The next step isn't another memo or hashtag. It's collective action to build a society where support comes without gag orders or hidden shackles. Community is mental-health liberation's unsung hero, praised in speeches, starved in budgets. Peer groups, intergenerational mentorship, grassroots art projects: they're the social glue no prescription can match. Isolation is the prison; connection is the solvent that dissolves it.

"Recovery" has been butchered into a sterile checkbox. True recovery is messy, non-linear, deeply human. You can live with schizophrenia and thrive running a company, raising kids, and writing books. Strengths-based policies don't just reframe individuals; they expand society's notion of what's possible.

The numbers are merciless: poor mental health costs over a trillion dollars globally in lost productivity, emergency care, and law-enforcement budgets swallowed by crises. Framing mental health as a human right is not utopian; it's smart economics. Nations investing in dignity, community, and strength don't just reduce suffering; they flourish.

Underfund mental health, then feign surprise when ERs, jails, and broken lives bear the cost. That's not oversight; it's policy. To break our chains, mental-health care must be treated as core infrastructure, not a luxury. Crisis shouldn't land you in a cell. We've outsourced care to police, built for punishment, not healing. The result: a revolving door of incarceration that deepens trauma. We need co-response teams, crisis-intervention units, and well-staffed community centers. These models halve arrests, slash hospital visits, and cut recurrences while fostering genuine care engagement.

Reform can't stop at prison bars. Jails and prisons can't treat complex clinical needs; they warehouse despair. Mandatory mental-health screening, treatment, and seamless re-entry support are non-negotiable. Jail-diversion programs cut recidivism. That's proof treatment outperforms punishment. Funnelling people into cages isn't evidence-poor; it's will-poor.

We must banish the paternalistic fantasy that experts know best without hearing from those they serve. Mental-health policies have long been drafted by administrators fluent in "patients" but deaf to lived voices. That ends now. People with lived experience must co-create, co-lead, and co-evaluate every program, research agenda, and budget. "Nothing about us without us" isn't a hashtag; it's quality control. When those who've navigated the system steer its design, engagement soars, outcomes improve, and dignity prevails.

There is no place for half-measures. A handful of "mental-health days," some motivational posters, and an annual pep rally, these are the gilded deck chairs on the sinking Titanic. We need radical empathy, fearless investment, relentless education, and merciless demolition of archaic systems so normal we barely notice them. Dark humour isn't a distraction; it's armour. If we can laugh at the Kafkaesque cruelty of "caring" bureaucracies that quietly lock people away, or we can face the harder work of tearing them down.

Data, lived experience, and creative resistance point in one direction: liberation is possible. Picture a world where asking for help earns applause; where recovery isn't a shameful secret; where no one is sentenced to a lifetime of silence because their brain works differently. The straitjackets are in plain sight, grotesque, absurd, indefensible. This time, we rip them off for good.

Chapter Twenty-One
Epilogue of Horrors

Welcome to the grand finale, where we finally admit what we've known for decades: our "helpful" mental-health systems are less comforting blankets and more gleeful obstacle courses. We've piled up every study imaginable, gathered hundreds of patient testaments, performed policy autopsies with the zeal of forensic pathologists and still prefer torture by bureaucracy to actual care. Nice work, humanity.

Click here to learn how to jump through our eligibility hoops! A maze that would make Kafka blush. Call our crisis line, please, if you don't mind waiting in eternal limbo on hold. We'll tell you to "reach out" and then penalize you for doing it wrong. We'll brand your agony as personal failure, issue you a guilt trip for free, and watch you sink while we busy ourselves perfecting refusal-to-help letters. This isn't ignorance. It's willful apathy masquerading as neutral policy.

Let's dispense with the myth of benevolent indifference. When you can't find a roof over your head, you rot. When care is inaccessible, your breakdown is front-page news, minus the rescue. When support is conditional, shame breeds like bacteria. Invisible straitjackets tighten not out of malice alone, but because we've learned to shrug at human suffering. Claiming compassion while shrugging is dishonest. Claiming neutrality while shackling people is downright cruel.

Here's the big lie: dignity can wait. First, you must "stabilize," "comply," "prove insight," or "earn trust," as though you're a lab rat in some perverse experiment. Reality check: dignity isn't a trophy to be unlocked after you've "improved." It's the soil where improvement grows. Without autonomy, safety, housing, and actual respect, you don't treat illness; you cultivate despair.

Sympathy is toothless without solidarity. Feeling bad for you is a performance, one we hide behind a curtain of good intentions. Real humanity shows up in actual budgets, laws, zoning approvals, hiring practices, in courtrooms and classrooms, in every emergency protocol that says, "People first." Not "People sometimes, if they pass inspection."

Brace yourself: doing this right will be terrifying. It means redistributing power, scrapping cherished myths like "mental illness only affects other people," and admitting the line between "us" and "them" is imaginary. Beyond straitjackets lies no utopia of pain-free living; it's a world where we refuse to abandon folks at their lowest ebb. A world where suffering is not a private tragedy but a collective call to arms. We'd measure success not by how quickly we can stuff people back under control, but by how much suffering we've prevented in the first place.

This is the call to humanity: not a cutesy slogan, but an unignorable demand to act. Systems are human-made, so they can be unmade. The question isn't "Can we do it?" but "Will we?" The cost of real care has never been too high; we've just been bankrupting ourselves on neglect.

Perfection? Forget it. We just need decency. We need to refuse a world where a person must be "broken enough" to merit help. Where the reflex is to doubt, minimize, or defer. Crisis shouldn't be the gateway to care; it should be the failure we fight to prevent. A humane society doesn't make you prove your pain or earn protection; it offers it as a right, as essential as clean water.

Look closely: the deadliest cruelty is bureaucratic, polite, and impeccably documented. It lives in referral loops, denial letters, eligibility thresholds, and "Not at this time." Naming it isn't radical; ignoring it is.

If this book has argued for anything, it's that mental health care is an ethical battleground. How we treat those in distress says everything about what we value: worth, responsibility, belonging. Investing in care is not a weakness; it's smart. Centring dignity is not naïveté, it's stability. Choosing compassion over containment is not recklessness; it's finally paying attention.

So, let's stop asking if we can afford to care. Let's ask how we ever justified not caring. Build pathways wide enough for everyone, timely, humane, and unconditional. Respond to vulnerability with support, not suspicion. Beyond invisible straitjackets isn't chaos, it's connection. It's lives not splintered by needless suffering. It's a future free of the "break then help" trap.

The evidence is clear, the stories painfully so. Responsibility lies with us. History will judge whether we insisted we didn't know or admitted we didn't care. The cost of inaction is not theoretical; it's suicides, stalled lives, families shattered, prisons overflowing. The cost of action is simply discomfort: funding commitments, political courage, the radical notion that human lives trump balance sheets.

As this saga ends, never to be shelved as "important but ignored," let it fuel reform, advocacy, and sustained discomfort. Mental health isn't a seasonal charity or a rhetorical accessory. It must be a priority. Every life matters, especially the inconvenient, the angry, the "difficult." Dismantling invisible straitjackets demands more than compassion or policy alone. It needs the gritty work of building systems that function for the people they serve.

Let this be our real commitment: systems that heal, not control; communities that support, not survey; a culture that sees mental health as a shared responsibility, not a personal failing. Prevent suffering before it becomes spectacle. Because in the end, society's measure isn't wealth or rhetoric; it's who it protects, who it sacrifices, and how much suffering it tolerates for the sake of convenience.

What we want isn't radical or naïve. It's simple: a world where stigma is optional, dignity is mandatory, and mental health care is treated like the infrastructure it is alongside roads, water, and fire services. A society that fosters empowerment instead of containment. Where people living with mental illness are seen as whole beings, not liabilities. Not anecdotes for fundraising galas, but experts whose lived experience informs policy, service design, and public narratives.

The call is urgent. The opportunity is real. The responsibility is ours. Stand with the suffering. Speak for the silenced. Act for lives on the edge. Together, we must demand a world where hope is fierce, care is a right, and human potential is unleashed. Anything less is complicity a continuation of the straitjacket.

Inaction costs lives: action, though uncomfortable, unlocks limitless power. Armed with empathy and determination, we can forge a world where no one is trapped by silence, shame, or neglect; where care, dignity, and hope are everyone's birthrights.

This is the world we demand. This is the future we claim. It begins now, with us, at this precipice. The invisible straitjackets can be dismantled, but only if we choose to do so.

No more excuses. No more straitjackets.

Glossary of Mental Health Terms and Diagnoses

Acute Stress Reaction – A short-term psychological response to a traumatic or stressful event, often including anxiety, confusion, or heightened arousal.

Agitation – A state of restlessness, irritability, or heightened emotional arousal that may interfere with daily functioning or safety.

Anhedonia – The inability to experience pleasure from activities usually found enjoyable, commonly associated with depression.

Anxiety Disorder – A group of mental health disorders characterized by excessive fear, worry, or nervousness that impairs daily life. Examples include Generalized Anxiety Disorder, Panic Disorder, and Social Anxiety Disorder.

Bipolar Disorder – A mental health condition characterized by alternating periods of depression and mania or hypomania.

Chronic Mental Illness – Long-lasting psychiatric disorders that significantly impair functioning over time, such as schizophrenia or severe bipolar disorder.

Clinical Depression / Major Depressive Disorder – A mood disorder involving persistent sadness, loss of interest in activities, fatigue, and impaired daily functioning.

Cognitive Behavioural Therapy (CBT) – A widely used therapeutic approach focusing on identifying and changing maladaptive thought patterns and behaviours.

Community-Based Mental Health Care – Services delivered in the community rather than in institutional settings, often including counselling, outreach, and rehabilitation programs.

Comorbidity – The co-occurrence of two or more disorders or medical conditions in the same individual.

Control Interventions – Measures used in psychiatric settings to manage acute patient behaviour, including physical restraint, seclusion, or chemical sedation.

Crisis Intervention – Immediate, short-term support provided to individuals experiencing a mental health emergency to stabilize their situation and prevent harm.

Delusions – False beliefs firmly held despite evidence to the contrary, often associated with psychotic disorders.

De-escalation – Techniques used by professionals to reduce agitation, aggression, or emotional distress without the use of force.

Dissociation – A mental process where a person disconnects from thoughts, feelings, memories, or a sense of identity, often as a coping mechanism for trauma.

Forensic Psychiatry / Forensic Psychiatric Unit – A branch of psychiatry focused on patients who have mental health disorders and have interacted with the criminal justice system.

Hallucinations – Sensory experiences without external stimuli, such as hearing voices or seeing things that are not present.

Inpatient Care – Mental health care provided in a hospital or residential facility where the patient stays overnight for treatment.

Involuntary Hospitalization – Admission to a psychiatric facility without the patient's consent, typically due to risk of harm to self or others.

Mania / Hypomania – Periods of elevated, expansive, or irritable mood, increased activity, or impulsivity; mania is more severe than hypomania.

Medication-Assisted Treatment (MAT) – Use of medications in combination with counselling and behavioural therapies to treat mental health or substance use disorders.

Obsessive-Compulsive Disorder (OCD) – A disorder marked by persistent, intrusive thoughts (obsessions) and repetitive behaviours or mental acts (compulsions) performed to reduce anxiety.

Outpatient Care – Mental health treatment provided while the patient lives at home, such as therapy sessions, counselling, or day programs.

Patient Rights – Legal and ethical protections afforded to individuals receiving mental health care, including the right to informed consent, privacy, and humane treatment.

Post-Traumatic Stress Disorder (PTSD) – A mental health condition following exposure to trauma, characterized by intrusive memories, hyperarousal, avoidance, and negative mood changes.

Psychiatric Evaluation / Assessment – Comprehensive evaluation by a mental health professional to diagnose mental health conditions and recommend treatment.

Psychosis – A condition involving impaired reality testing, often with hallucinations, delusions, or disorganized thinking.

Restraint / Seclusion – Physical, mechanical, or chemical methods used in psychiatric settings to limit a patient's movement for safety; considered a last resort.

Schizoaffective Disorder – A mental health disorder featuring symptoms of both schizophrenia (psychosis) and mood disorder (depression or mania).

Schizophrenia – A chronic psychiatric disorder involving psychosis, disorganized thinking, impaired functioning, and negative symptoms such as social withdrawal or flat affect.

Self-Harm / Non-Suicidal Self-Injury (NSSI) – The deliberate infliction of harm to one's own body without intent to die, often as a coping mechanism.

Suicidal Ideation – Thoughts or preoccupations with ending one's life, which may or may not involve a plan.

Trauma-Informed Care – An approach to mental health treatment that recognizes the prevalence of trauma and emphasizes safety, trustworthiness, and empowerment.

Voluntary Hospitalization – Admission to a psychiatric facility with the patient's informed consent, typically for assessment, treatment, or stabilization.

References

American Psychiatric Association. (2013). *Diagnostic and statistical manual of mental disorders* (5th ed.). American Psychiatric Association Publishing.

Andersen, C., et al. (2017). Applying sensory modulation to mental health inpatient care. *Archives of Psychiatric Nursing, 31*(3), 272–278. https://pubmed.ncbi.nlm.nih.gov/28719249

Province of British Columbia, Ministry of Health. (2025). *Standards and guidelines for secure rooms in designated mental health facilities under the BC Mental Health Act* [PDF]. Government of British Columbia. https://www2.gov.bc.ca/assets/gov/health/managing-your-health/mental-health-substance-use/secure-rooms-standards-guidelines.pdf

Barbic, S. P., Honer, W. G., & Durisko, Z. (2017). A calming space: How sensory modulation rooms can help reduce distress in acute psychiatric care. *Journal of Psychiatric and Mental Health Nursing, 24*(8), 538–546. https://doi.org/10.1111/jpm.12412

Canadian Institute for Health Information. (2023). *Control interventions in mental health hospital care in Canada*. CIHI. https://www.cihi.ca/en/mental-health

Canadian Mental Health Association, Ontario. (2023). *A quarter of hospitalized mental health patients restrained: New CIHI data.* https://ontario.cmha.ca/news/a-quarter-of-hospitalized-mental-health-patients-restrained

Chapleau, A., Harrison, J., Love, S., & Sherman, D. (2023). Mental health outcomes before psychotropic medications: A retrospective case series of one state hospital, 1945–1954. *BMC Health Services Research, 23*, 257. https://doi.org/10.1186/s12913-023-09235-8

Chow, W. S., & Priebe, S. (2013). Understanding psychiatric institutionalization: A conceptual review. *BMC Psychiatry, 13*, 169. https://doi.org/10.1186/1471-244X-13-169

Coldwell, C. M., & Bender, W. S. (2007). The effectiveness of assertive community treatment for homeless individuals with severe mental illness.

American Journal of Psychiatry, 164(3), 393–399. https://doi.org/10.1176/ajp.2007.164.3.393

Costain, E. (2025). Replacing seclusion & restraint practices in psychiatry with sensory rooms. *Columbia Social Work Review, 23*(1), 5–27. https://journals.library.columbia.edu/index.php/cswr/article/view/13173

Cummings, K. S., Grandfield, S. A., & Coldwell, C. M. (2010). Caring with comfort rooms: Reducing seclusion and restraint use in psychiatric facilities. *Journal of Psychosocial Nursing and Mental Health Services, 48*(6), 26–30. https://doi.org/10.3928/02793695-20100503-02

Daguman, E. I. V. (2023). Uncovering complexities in reducing aggression, conflict, and restrictive practices in psychiatric inpatient settings. *International Journal of Mental Health Nursing, 32*(3), 864–875. https://doi.org/10.1111/inm.13376

Drake, R. E., Bond, G. R., & Becker, D. R. (2012). *Individual placement and support: An evidence-*

based approach to supported employment. Oxford University Press.

Drake, R. E., & Latimer, E. (2012). Lessons learned in developing community mental health care in North America. *World Psychiatry, 11*(1), 47–51. https://www.ncbi.nlm.nih.gov/pmc/articles/PMC3266763/

Fairweather Lodge. (n.d.). In *Wikipedia*. https://en.wikipedia.org/wiki/Fairweather_Lodge

Fields, E., Farmer, E. M. Z., Apperson, J., Mustillo, S., & Simmers, D. (2006). Treatment and post-treatment effects of residential treatment using a re-education model. *Behavioural Disorders, 31*(3), 312–322.

Fountain House. (n.d.). In *Wikipedia*. https://en.wikipedia.org/wiki/Fountain_House_(nonprofit_organization)

Frontiers in Psychiatry. (2024). Seclusion and mechanical restraint in the wake of the COVID-19 pandemic. *Frontiers in Psychiatry*. https://www.frontiersin.org/journals/psychiatry/articles/10.3389/fpsyt.2024.1428599/full

Gerritsen, R., Kok, R., & Veldhuizen, S. (2023). *Protocols to reduce seclusion in inpatient mental health units: A systematic review.* National Center for Biotechnology Information. https://www.ncbi.nlm.nih.gov/books/NBK599803

Goulet, M. H., Larue, C., Dumais, A., & Villeneuve, E. (2024). Seclusion and mechanical restraint in a Canadian psychiatric hospital before and after the COVID-19 pandemic. *Frontiers in Psychiatry, 15*, Article 1428599. https://doi.org/10.3389/fpsyt.2024.1428599

Happell, B., Moxham, L., & Platania-Phung, C. (2015). Trauma-informed care in inpatient mental health settings: A review of the literature. *Issues in Mental Health Nursing, 36*(9), 697–705. https://doi.org/10.3109/01612840.2015.1025079

Hirdes, J. P., et al. (2015). Restraint and confinement still an everyday practice in mental health settings. *Healthcare Management Forum.*

Huckshorn, K. A. (2004). Reducing seclusion and restraint use in mental health settings: Core strategies for prevention. *Journal of Psychosocial Nursing and Mental Health Services, 42*(9), 22–33.

Insel, T. R., & Quirion, R. (2005). Psychiatry as a clinical neuroscience discipline. *JAMA, 294*(17), 2221–2224.

Kim, B., et al. (2023). Association of homelessness and psychiatric hospital readmission: A retrospective cohort study. *BMC Psychiatry, 23*, 459.

Lamb, H. R., & Bachrach, L. L. (2001). Some perspectives on deinstitutionalization. *Psychiatric Services, 52*(8), 1039–1045.

Lamb, H. R., & Weinberger, L. E. (2005). The shift of psychiatric inpatient care from hospitals to criminal justice settings. *Journal of the American Academy of Psychiatry and the Law, 33*(4), 529–534.

Larue, C., Dumais, A., Ahern, E., Bernheim, E., & Mailhot, M.-P. (2009). Factors influencing decisions on seclusion and restraint. *Journal of Psychiatric and Mental Health Nursing, 16*(5), 440–446. https://doi.org/10.1111/j.1365-2850.2009.01396.x

LeBel, J., & Goldstein, R. (2005). The economic cost of using restraint and seclusion in mental health facilities. *Psychiatric Services, 56*(9), 1109–1114. https://doi.org/10.1176/appi.ps.56.9.1109

McCann, T. V., McKenna, H., & Smith, M. (2013). The experience of seclusion and restraint in psychiatric settings: Perspectives of patients. *Journal of Psychiatric and Mental Health Nursing, 20*(8), 569–577.

Mechanic, D. (2014). The deinstitutionalization movement: Lessons learned and implications for policy and practice. *Social Psychiatry and Psychiatric Epidemiology, 49*(10), 1461–1464.

Mechanic, D., McAlpine, D. D., & Rochefort, D. A. (2013). *Mental health and social policy: Beyond managed care* (6th ed.). Pearson.

Morrison, E. F., & Lehane, D. (1995). Restraint and seclusion: A review of the literature. *Journal of Psychiatric and Mental Health Nursing, 2*(2), 113–120.

Nelson, G., & MacLeod, T. (2017). Housing programs for people with serious mental illness. In J. Sylvestre, G. Nelson, & T. Aubry (Eds.), *Housing, citizenship, and communities for people with serious mental illness: Theory, research, practice, and policy perspectives* (pp. 155–185). Oxford University Press.

National Institute of Mental Health. (2023). *Mental health medications.* U.S. Department of Health and Human Services. https://www.nimh.nih.gov/health/topics/mental-health-medications

National Mental Health Act of 1946, Pub. L. No. 79-487, 42 U.S.C. § 201 (1946).

Oostermeijer, S., Spreeuwenberg, M., Dekker, J., & Bulten, E. (2021). Design features that reduce the use of seclusion and restraint in mental health facilities: A rapid systematic review. *BMJ Open, 11*(7), e046647.

Perryman, B. (2025). Regulating restraint: Legal oversight of seclusion in Canadian forensic psychiatric hospitals. *Canadian Journal of Law and Society, 40*(2).

Rosenhan, D. L. (1973). On being sane in insane places. *Science, 179*(4070), 250–258. https://doi.org/10.1126/science.179.4070.250

Saks, E. R. (2002). Refusing care: Forced treatment and the rights of the mentally ill. *University of Chicago Law Review, 69*(2), 571–609.

Shorter, E. (1997). *A history of psychiatry: From the era of the asylum to the age of Prozac*. Wiley.

Standing Senate Committee on Social Affairs, Science and Technology. (2004). *Out of the shadows at last: Transforming mental health, mental illness and addiction services in Canada.*

Statistics Canada. (2009). *Mental health and the criminal justice system — Overview of issues.*

Straitjacket. (n.d.). In *Wikipedia.* https://en.wikipedia.org/wiki/Straitjacket

Sussman, S. (2017). The history of mental health services in Canada. *Madridge Journal of Internal and Emergency Medicine, 1*(1), 7–13.

Sussman, S. (2018). Psychiatry in Ontario and throughout Canada in the twentieth century. *Madridge Journal of Internal and Emergency Medicine, 2*(1), 40–44.

Sweeney, S., Filson, B., Kennedy, A., Collinson, L., & Gillard, S. (2023). Use of sensory rooms in adult psychiatric inpatient settings: A systematic review and narrative synthesis. *International Journal of Mental Health Systems*.

Thompson, G., McGarry, D., & Lee, D. (2021). Design features that reduce the use of seclusion and restraint in mental health facilities: A systematic review. *BMJ Open, 11*(7), e046647.

Torrey, E. F. (2014). *American psychosis: How the federal government destroyed the mental illness treatment system*. Oxford University Press.

Tsemberis, S., & Eisenberg, R. F. (2000). Pathways to housing: Supported housing for street dwellers with psychiatric disabilities. *Psychiatric Services, 51*(4), 487–493.

United States Substance Abuse and Mental Health Services Administration. (2014). *Trauma-informed care in behavioural health services* (Treatment Improvement Protocol Series No. 57).

Wasser, T., Strockbine, B., Uyanwune, Y., & Kapoor, R. (2023). Restraint and seclusion practices and policies in U.S. forensic psychiatric hospitals. *Journal of the American Academy of Psychiatry and the Law, 51*(4), 566–574.

Whitaker, R. (2010). *Anatomy of an epidemic: Magic bullets, psychiatric drugs, and the astonishing rise of mental illness in America*. Crown Publishing Group.

Wright, S., Stewart, D., & Bowers, L. (2019). The use of sensory rooms in psychiatric inpatient care: A systematic review. *International Journal of Mental Health Nursing, 28*(2), 352–365.

Wykes, T., & Callard, F. (2010). What is the history of realignment in psychiatric care systems? *History of Psychiatry, 21*(2), 173–189.

"What if I fall?"

"Oh, but my darling, what if you Fly?"

Erin Hanson

www.ingramcontent.com/pod-product-compliance
Lightning Source LLC
Chambersburg PA
CBHW071433230926
51846CB00001B/218
9781990426261